ROYAL SCHOOL
of NEEDLEWORK
EMBROIDERY TECHNIQUES

ROYAL SCHOOL
of NEEDLEWORK
EMBROIDERY TECHNIQUES

TEXT BY SALLY SAUNDERS
DESIGNS BY ANNE BUTCHER AND DEBRA BARRETT

B.T. Batsford Ltd, London

ACKNOWLEDGEMENTS

My thanks to my family for all their support. My particular thanks to Elizabeth Elvin for asking me to write this book, and for her patience and encouragement.

Also my thanks go to all who have worked in the workrooms of the Royal School of Needlework to produce so many original embroideries, to encourage a range of abilities and tastes exclusively for the readers of this book.

Thanks also go to Anne Butcher and Debra Barrett for their work on designs and to Julie Lampitt, Jayne Bleby and Melissa Cheeseman for all the typing and checking involved.

Thanks also go to the British Museum for the use of photographs of Elizabeth I's seal purse and the Worshipful Company of Girdlers for the photographs of their crown.

First published 1998 by
B T Batsford Ltd
583 Fulham Road
London SW6 5BY
in association with RSN Enterprises Ltd
for the
Royal School of Needlework
Apartment 12A, Hampton Court Palace
Surrey KT8 9AU
Registered Charity No. 312774

ISBN 0 7134 8401 2

Printed in Hong Kong

Illustrations by Penny Brown
Photography by Michael Wicks
Designed by DWN Ltd London

Batsford Books Online: www.batsford.com

CONTENTS

INTRODUCTION

The Royal School of Needlework was founded in 1872 by Princess Christian of Schleswig-Holstein, Queen Victoria's third daughter. The School's original aim was to preserve hand embroidery as an art form, following the introduction of crude and poorly worked machine-made textiles. Princess Christian and her friends also wished to provide an acceptable form of employment for women of gentle birth who, in the wake of the Industrial Revolution, found themselves in great financial need.

Members of the Arts and Crafts Movement, William Morris, Sir Edward Burne-Jones, Walter Crane and later May Morris, all helped the Royal School bring about a revival of simple good design and quality materials and workmanship. Their influence and designs still remain to the present day.

Lady Marion Alford, first Vice-President of the School, comments in her book *Needlework as Art* (1886) that 'Millions have enjoyed the art of needle for thousands of years, and it will continue to be a solace and a delight as long as the world lasts; like all Art it gives the ever new joy of Creation.' This sentiment is still true today and the Royal School of Needlework continues its founding traditions, training students and apprentices to the highest standards.

Each year six apprentices start an intensive three-year training, during which they learn every aspect of decorative hand embroidery, design restoration and conservation. The Royal School also offers a range of courses, varying in length from one day to one year, for external students.

The School has been privileged to enjoy the continuing patronage of members of the Royal Family, including Queen Alexandra, Queen Mary and Princess Alice of Athlone. Queen Elizabeth, the Queen Mother, is the School's current Patron and its President is the Duchess of Gloucester.

The aim of this book is to pass on the Royal School of Needlework's methods for working a variety of basic embroidery techniques. We hope to encourage those who love embroidery, but who may need help and inspiration to take on new projects.

Start with a small piece of your chosen technique so that you can explore it thoroughly and any difficulties encountered can be sorted out before moving on to something larger. When you feel confident with this technique, try adding it to other pieces of work, mixing your techniques if appropriate.

Silk shading can look wonderful added to many other types of embroidery. Try working it separately, then pad it and apply to canvas work. Goldwork techniques always look rich on any piece of embroidery that will not have a lot of wear and tear. Blackwork could be worked on coloured evenweave in a colour. Try working some of the simplest patterns over waste canvas on any fabric. Crewel work fillings look wonderful on a space dyed background fabric. Beads and gold thread could be added to some of the patterns.

For embroiderers with some knowledge of machine embroidery, beautiful backgrounds can be created and these lovely hand-embroidered techniques could be included to give wonderful, textured rich pieces of embroidery.

Elizabeth Elvin
Principal

Royal Coat of Arms (90 x 70 cm/35½ x 27½ inches) from the RSN Collection, worked in silk and gold threads on a silk and velvet ground by staff and apprentices of the Royal School of Needlework (1994).

Each element was worked separately and individually padded using a variety of materials, including soft string, cotton, felt and carpet felt. Metal threads of gold and silver were applied to the padding using methods of couching and chipwork. The Lion and Unicorn are couched in gold and silver Passing, the mantle and crest are worked in Passing and detailed in Pearl Purl and Bright Check. Areas of silk shading were worked for the hillock centre shield and the detail on the crowns, helm and mantle. On completion, each element was applied to the velvet to achieve the final three-dimensional effect.

PREPARING FOR AN EMBROIDERY PROJECT

Before embroidery can begin, a great deal of thought must be given to the various elements involved in the preparation.

FABRICS

Choose good quality fabrics, which are a generous size for your project. Check there are no dirty marks or flaws on the fabric and always inspect the centre fold carefully to make sure this is not dusty or damaged by being folded for a long time. When choosing fabrics it is a good idea to have a small second piece of fabric large enough to go into a ring frame; this will be useful for trying out stitches and effects. It may be appropriate to dye your own fabric, or you can buy small pieces of space dyed material from specialist suppliers. These make lovely and very original backgrounds.

When the fabric has been chosen, it should be pressed with a steam iron and then rolled on to a cardboard roll ready for use. If the material is fine it will need to be backed to give it more body. This backing fabric should be washed to shrink it first. When damp dry it should be ironed and put on to a cardboard roll to await use. If fabric is not shrunk first puckering can occur between the sections of embroidery when the work is finished.

THREADS

The choice of threads obviously depends on the technique to be carried out. It is a good idea to store your threads in clean polythene sweet jars in ranges of colours. This helps you see at a glance the threads you have available. This method is particularly useful for a technique like blackwork or whitework where you need a range of threads in different thicknesses. These threads could include all types of embroidery threads along with reels and cops of cotton, silks and synthetic threads.

Metal threads must, of course, be stored in airtight tins in a generous amount of acid-free white or black tissue. Because this makes it difficult to see what threads you have, it is a good idea to make a pattern card of all your threads and keep it on the top of your tin so you can see at a glance the threads available, and any extras you may need to buy. Gold thread should be handled as little as possible to prevent damage and tarnishing. Lurex threads, of course, could also be stored in a jar as these will be unaffected by handling.

DESIGN

There are many useful books on how to produce design for embroidery and a list is included at the back of this book. It is much better to take advice from design books than to turn to other people's embroideries as a source of inspiration. They have probably taken their design as far as it can reasonably go, and it is always unfair to copy other embroiderers' ideas. Instead, go back to the real design sources, looking at flowers, animals, fruit, vegetables and trees. Textiles and architecture are a wonderful fount of ideas. Look at shell patterns and butterfly wings to find interesting patterns to inspire you. Make sketches of the areas you like; try enlarging these sketches and isolating a section with a window mount. Now trace the design lines inside the mount. Try repeating this tracing. You will find that enlarging the design is also helpful.

You may be surprised at your results. When you have your design, make a good accurate copy on heavyweight tracing paper.

TOOLS

As professional embroiderers at the Royal School of Needlework, we nearly all invest in a tool box or fishing box. These are light to carry to classes and have a wonderful range of little compartments in which to put all the various things an embroiderer needs. We always have in our boxes a range of needles of every shape and size, including large bracing needles; scissors, small sharp ones for thread, a small pair for gold thread only, paper scissors and scissors for cutting fabric; beeswax; tape measure; thimbles; pencils, rubbers and rulers; a pair of compasses; dressmaking pins, glasshead pins and drawing pins; masking tape; a pot of powdered charcoal and cuttlefish; pricker; button thread for framing up and a ball of string; dumpy screwdriver for loosening screws on ring frames; a tiny baby's hairbrush to remove unwanted pieces of gold thread from work; a 10 cm (4 inch) square board covered in velvet for cutting gold thread on; a thick duster – this can be folded up to prick designs on, or used to remove pounce from the fabric or pricking.

Many other little things you use from time to time can also be included, such as tacking cotton, a small pot of PVA glue, stiletto for white work, dissolvable fabric and a small ring frame, about 10-15 cm (4-6 inches) for trying out stitches. The bigger the box the more we all find we must have in our box!

SQUARE FRAMES AND FRAMING UP

One of the most important ingredients for successful embroidery is careful framing up on a square frame. The size of the frame depends on the project to be undertaken. It is wise to avoid the frames with screw fastenings as these are impossible to tighten satisfactorily. The professional square peg frames will give the best results and will keep your work clean, fresh and unpuckered.

Background fabric will be chosen to work with each technique. Some will need backing and some won't. Details are given for two methods here and each technique will refer you to which method to use.

The size of the background material should be the

size of the finished project plus 10-15 cm (4–6 inches) turning allowance for mounting or making up the piece when the embroidery is complete. Cut the fabric by the grain and press with a steam iron or damp cloth.

Backing cotton material should be preshrunk by washing first before cutting out. Allow 12 mm (½ inch) turnings on all sides of the fabric for stitching to the frame. Cut the fabric by the grain.

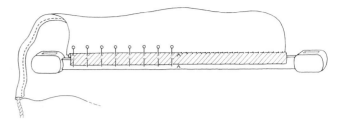

Fig.2 *Pin the turnings to the webbing then oversew from the centre.*

Method A:
Framing up Work Without a Backing

1   Fold a 12 mm (½ inch) turning top and bottom of the fabric. Stitch string down the sides like a piping cord over 12 mm (½ inch) turning or attach webbing

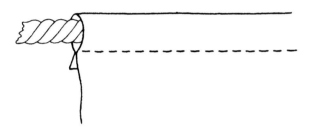

Fig.1 *Stitch string down the sides as with piping cord.*

down the sides with upright tacking (see Fig. 1).

2   Mark the centre of the webbing on the frame with a pin. Mark the top and bottom turnings of the background fabric with a pin.

3   Put the 12 mm (½ inch) turnings to the webbing and pin (see Fig. 2).

4   Oversew all along the webbing with stitches no more than 3 mm (⅛ inch) deep (see Fig. 2). Start in the centre and work out to avoid material walking along the webbing. Fasten off by working back over stitches for 2 cm (¾ inch) and then cut the thread.

5   Place the arms through the bars and tighten the frame by positioning the pegs.

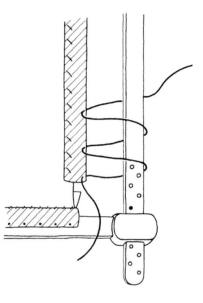

Fig.3 *Brace the frame with string.*

6   When the frame is tight brace with string (see Fig. 3) threaded into a large bracing needle. Work down through the edge of the fabric, never up, to avoid accidents. Use string from a ball to give a continual length. Leave 45 cm (18 inches) each end to fasten off with a slip knot (see Figs. 5a and 5b). This knot allows you to retighten the frame quickly when it becomes spongy when embroidery is under way.

If the background is fine and needs backing, use Method B.

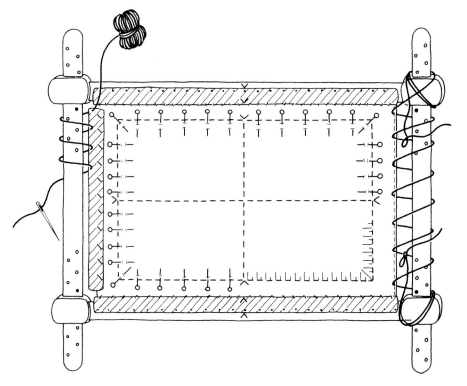

Fig. 4 Using a slack frame, pin the background fabric to the calico. Stitch from the corner of the drawn thread in a long and short stitch.

Method B:
Framing Up With a Backing Fabric

7   If a fine background fabric is used, mount the preshrunk backing cotton as already described in steps 1-6 but do not tighten the frame or string.

8   Fold the background fabric in half both ways and mark the centre with pins. Tack centre lines across the fabric.

9   About 12 mm (½ inch) from the webbing, draw a thread in the backing fabric and one at right angles 2.5 cm (1 inch) beside the string (or webbing).

10 Place the background on to the slack frame, lining up the edge of the fabric with the two drawn threads in backing fabric. Pin in position.

11 Thread up some cotton or suitable thread and start to stitch from the corner of the drawn thread along the webbing edge in a long and short stitch (see Fig. 4). When complete, work along the string edge, lining up the edge of the background fabric to second drawn thread. Stitch in long and short stitches. Now complete the stitching on the other two sides in the same way, smoothing the material out and checking with a tape measure that the fabric is quite square.

12 Tighten the pegs and string so that the fabrics are now drum tight. Fasten with a slip knot (see Figs. 5a and 5b).

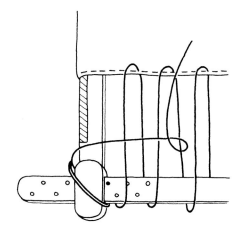

Fig. 5a Fasten off with a slip knot (1st stage).

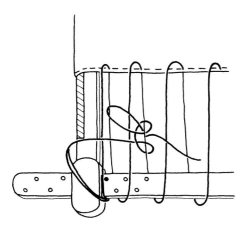

Fig.5b Fasten off with a slip knot (2nd stage).

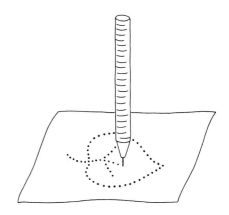

Fig.6 Hold the pin vice upright and prick the design lines.

TRANSFERRING A DESIGN ON TO FABRIC

There are several different ways of transferring a design on to background fabric, and the method chosen is influenced by the type of embroidery to be carried out. A free design may not always look good with outlines and solid embroidery throughout, in which case a different way of transferring a design would be more appropriate.

Method A: Prick and Pounce

1   Take a sheet of good quality tracing paper at least 5 cm (2 inches) larger than the design to be traced. Mark in pencil the centre of the paper both down and across.

2   Position over the design, matching the centre lines. Trace the design with a fine, well drawn line.

3   Lay the traced design over a folded duster.

4   With a pin vice and a no. 9 needle, prick all the design lines with a series of holes very close together but not so close that they tear the tracing paper (see Fig. 6). Check all the lines have been pricked by holding the tracing paper up to the light.

5   Now lay the pricked design on the material in the frame, matching up the centre tack and pencil lines.

6   Place books under the frame to give a firm surface to paint the design on to the background. Weight the corners of the design to prevent movement.

7   Take a pot of appropriately coloured pounce. Black is powdered charcoal, white is powdered cuttlefish and together they will give a grey pounce. For your project use whichever pounce will show up on your background fabric.

8   Make a pad for applying the chosen pounce from a 6 x 15 cm (2½ x 6 inch) piece of felt. The felt is rolled up and stitched to form a pad. Dip this pad in the pounce very lightly and transfer the pounce on to your design, using a circular movement (see Fig. 7). Rub the pounce very gently over your design, covering each line once.

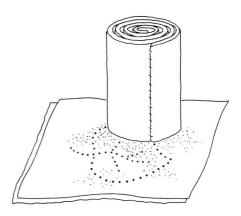

Fig.7 Rub pounce through the pricking using the felt pad.

9   When the design has been covered with the pounce pad, very carefully lift the corners of the design one at a time to check the design is showing clearly. When you are sure the design is showing clearly, remove the pricked design and clean with a soft tissue. This can then be stored for use again if needed. Gently blow off any excess pounce on the work.

10 Choose an appropriate watercolour paint. Use either black, white, grey or pale blue, depending on the background colour, making sure the paint will show but will not be too obvious and difficult to cover. Using a fine paintbrush (size 1), paint with a very fine line on all the pounced lines (see Fig. 8). If some of the lines are to be removed later in the working, these could be tacked rather than painted, and the tacks can be removed when the work is completed.

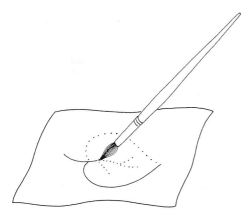

Fig.8 *Paint over the pounce lines with a fine paintbrush.*

11 When all the lines are transferred with paint lines on to the background fabric, take a clean folded duster and remove the remaining pounce by banging the back and front of the frame.

12 With a fine thread that matches the background material and a no. 9 crewel needle, tack the design through the backing and background, using stab stitch – a tiny stitch on the surface and a larger stitch

on the back, approximately 12 mm (½ inch). This process is to stop the two fabrics puckering when areas of heavy embroidery are carried out. You are now ready to start the embroidery.

Method B: Using Tissue Paper

Some designs, like blackwork designs, may not look right with outlines round all areas and if the design is painted on, these lines will have to be covered with stitching. In these cases it would be better to use the tissue paper method.

1   Frame up the material.

2   Trace the design very carefully on to tissue paper.

3   Lay the tissue paper tracing on to the fabric matching your centre tack lines with the centre design lines. Pin all round.

4   With a tacking thread stitch carefully along all the lines, starting and finishing the thread securely (see Fig. 9).

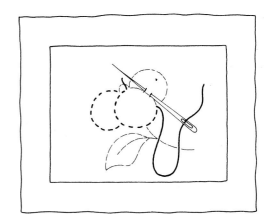

Fig.9 *Tack the traced design carefully through the tissue paper and background fabric using small stitches.*

5   When all the lines have been covered, tear the tissue paper away carefully leaving the tacked outline of the design showing on the fabric.

Method C: Using a Light Box

For some techniques, like whitework, it is a good idea to use a light box if possible. This means you will not have the worry of pounce on delicate fine white fabric.

1   Trace the design on to tracing paper using a fine permanent black pen.

2   Switch the light box on and place the design on top. Place the fabric on top, matching the centre lines with the centre tack lines. Place two weights each side of the design to prevent movement.

3   Trace the design with a fine paintbrush (see Fig. 10). If your project is whitework, use pale blue watercolour paint and a very fine line, or a well sharpened, good quality pale blue crayon used for watercolouring used dry.

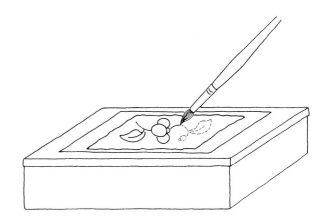

Fig. 10 Place the design on the light box with the fabric on top and then paint the design lines on the fabric.

INTRODUCING SILK SHADING

The production of silk is known to have been carried out for over 4,000 years and a great deal of silk fabric was being produced in China around 250 BC, although in strict secrecy. Some of the early Chinese garments were embroidered with rows of shaded chain stitch. At the same time as the Chinese were producing and decorating silk, the

A silk shaded garland of flowers, eighteenth century, RSN Collection

Egyptians in the fourth century were embroidering their linen. The early Egyptian Copts were Christians, and had a very important influence on the textiles of the time. Most of the work done was a weaving technique, but some of the roundels found on the remains of Coptic tunics included some beautifully worked silk shaded embroideries, an example of which is called the 'Apostles' and can be seen in the Victoria and Albert Museum.

Christianity came to Britain in the fourth century and with it came books and manuscripts, and these in turn were to influence the embroidery of the Middle Ages. In AD 909 a stole and maniple were made for St Cuthbert and were found later in his tomb. Some of the figures featured on these relics show draperies worked in rows of shaded split and stem stitch. (They can now be seen at Durham Cathedral.)

The *Opus Anglicanum* (English work) period or the eleventh to the fourteenth centuries was a wonderful era for professionally produced embroideries from abbeys and monasteries. These were quite often large items of solid embroidery worked mostly in underside couching. The designs were complicated interlaced geometric shapes known as quatre foils, in which were set various religious figures. The hair and draperies of these figures were often worked in rows of shaded split stitch, which produced a rather regimented form of shading.

After the dissolution of the monasteries by Henry VIII the great period of church embroidery came to an end in England, although it continued on the Continent for some years. In Britain the Tudor period brought

about some really magnificent embroideries for dress, and for the furnishings of the great houses that were built at that time; many had their own workrooms and embroiderers. Pattern books were printed to inspire workers. The designs were mostly natural flowers, animals and birds incorporated into designs of scrolling stems. These pieces of embroidery often included some beautiful shaded long and short stitch in a range of coloured silks. The items made were varied; for the home there were cushions, quilts, firescreens and hangings; for dress there were aprons, skirts, gloves, shoes, jackets, waistcoats, hats and purses. Wonderful examples of these can be seen in the Victoria and Albert Museum.

The end of the Tudor period saw the reduction in the size of houses, and therefore smaller furnishings were needed. The beds were now hung with Chinoiserie embroidered silk hangings. The large tapestries were replaced with embroidered panels, often worked in silk shading. This whole period was influenced by the increase in trade with the Far East. The rich embroideries on the clothes of the Tudor period were

A part embroidered stumpwork mirror showing silk shading, seventeenth century, RSN Collection.

replaced by plain satin decorated with needle-made lace cuffs and collars.

Embroidery in the Stuart period saw the introduction of stumpwork and Jacobean embroidery. Silk shading was quite often found on the flat areas of stumpwork boxes and mirrors, and Jacobean, although worked in wools, included enormous areas of long and short shading, one of the most famous examples being the bed curtains worked by Abigail Pett, now in the Victoria and Albert Museum.

The eighteenth century saw the introduction of embroidered classical pictures often worked by schoolgirls. The designs were taken from engravings, and the long and short stitch used gave the work a painted quality. The faces and hands were usually painted on the silk background first. The subject of these pieces nearly always included a figure of a lady often paying homage at a tomb; this type of work was known as needlepainting. The costume of this period included

Silkwork anemones, worked by a First Year Apprentice,
Harriet Lewis, 1997

some wonderful examples of silk shading. Embroidery
was worked on the fabric and then sold to dressmakers
and tailors, to be used in the clothes they produced.
Beautifully embroidered aprons and long waistcoats
included a lot of long and short stitch.

All kinds of different techniques and styles were
developed in the nineteenth century. Berlin woolwork
was probably the most popular embroidery for the
average embroiderer. The second half of the century saw
the first signs of the development of the individual
embroiderers. Designers like Harriet Wyatt, William
Morris and Edward Burne-Jones helped to encourage

embroidery. Schools and guilds were formed to promote
the craft. The Royal School of Needlework was founded
in 1872 and the students were taught a range of
embroidery techniques, among them long and short silk
shading, a technique for which the school is well known
even today. Morris and Burne-Jones were designers at
the School and a lot of their work included shading.

Long and short silk shading has been kept alive at
the Royal School of Needlework during the twentieth
century. Sadly it is not so often seen in other schools
and colleges. It is hoped that this book will inspire other
embroiderers to use this technique in a modern way, in
conjunction perhaps with machine embroidery and
fabric manipulation on hand-dyed fabrics.

A spray of flowers worked in silk shading by the Jones sisters who trained at the RSN between 1916 and 1918. They subsequently worked in the School's church workrooms for another 48 years on commissions including the Coronation robes of both H.M. Queen Elizabeth, The Queen Mother and H.M. Queen Elizabeth II.

Silk shaded parrot tulip, early twentieth century, RSN Collection.

METHODS OF SILK SHADING

Shading gives movement and life to a piece of embroidery and it is well worth trying to master this beautiful and satisfying technique. Shading can be achieved in various ways, for example with the layering of sheer fabrics, or with the use of stitches like French knots, detached chain stitch and seeding. These stitches can be used in a dot effect, using a change in shade or adjusting the closeness of the stitches. Line stitches like chain stitch, buttonhole stitch, herringbone stitch, stem stitch and split stitch can be worked in rows, changing the shade of the thread on each row.

Shading techniques include tent stitch on canvas, laid work and block shading (for silk and crewel work) and silk shading. This last technique, using long and short stitch worked in silk or cotton threads, is explored in this chapter.

This chapter is intended to stimulate more embroiderers to try this technique which over hundreds of years has been used to enhance many beautiful embroideries. So often the working of the technique is incorrectly described in embroidery books, and over the years this has made it difficult, if not impossible, for students to learn. We hope that after studying this book, long and short shading will give the same pleasure to you as it does to all who train at the Royal School of Needlework. Be prepared to practise this technique well because practice really does help to make perfect. Like anything we learn there are ground rules, but as you gain confidence, you will be able to experiment and develop the basic techniques you have learnt. Changing the colours and shades as you want to, mixing shades in the needle and just learning to paint with your needles will all come over time.

The background for silk shading can be varied. All types of silk complement the technique including hand-dyed fabrics sold for fabric colouring. The silk can be dip dyed, sponged, tie dyed, space dyed or microwave dyed - all will produce a different look to your work. Some design areas could be coloured with markle sticks, brushing the markle dye over a stencil to give silhouettes in some areas of the design. The background silk could be textured on the machine before the long and short is carried out.

Having made your decision on the background fabric, it will almost certainly need backing with some preshrunk cotton fabric to withstand the close stitching needed with this technique.

Long and short or tapestry shading can be carried out in a deep-sided ring frame, but will probably be most satisfactory mounted on a square peg frame (see page 10).

To trace the design on to the background, any of the three methods on pages 13-15 can be used but the most usual will be the prick and pounce method (see page 13). This will allow the fine detail of a design to be transferred accurately.

The needles used will be influenced by the scale of the shading carried out. Nos. 8, 9 or 10 crewel needles should be suitable for most projects.

Once the design is painted on to the background, the cotton backing and silk should be tacked together with a small stab stitch on the paint line every 12 mm (½ inch) using a fine sewing thread the colour of the background. This will prevent the silk walking on the cotton backing when the heavy embroidery is carried out.

Silk and tapestry shading can be worked in any stranded threads. Long and short is also a large feature of crewel work and is included in the crewel work chapter of this book where, of course, it is worked in wools rather than silk.

Working Instructions for Long and Short Stitch

There are two ways of working long and short stitch. The first is called tapestry shading and is worked only with the grain of the background fabric and in no other direction. When finished this technique has the same appearance as a tapestry, hence its name. This technique is useful when embroidering figures and similar subjects.

The second is directional long and short stitch. This is worked following the growing formation of a motif, such as a flower, leaf or feather.

Tapestry Shading

1   Work the underneath areas of the design first. Make a chart of the design and number the order of working. On the edge of the area to be worked stitch a row of split stitch. This gives a good edge to the work and should always be used to raise one design edge over another.

2   Long and short is then used in the first area of the design. Bring the needle up in the work and take it down over the split stitch. Work a row of stitches alternately long and short. The short stitches are two-thirds the length of the long stitches (see Fig. 1).

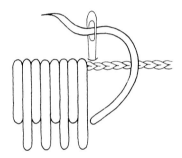

Fig. 1 In shading the short stitches are two-thirds the length of the long stitches.

3   After the first row all the stitches are of a similar length. The long and short stitches of the first row are now lengthened, bringing the needle up in the end of the first row of stitches splitting them and working a second row of stitches (see Figs. 2 and 3). While learning you could work into the short stitches first, then the long ones.

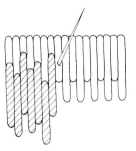

Fig. 2 Now lengthen the long and short stitches of the first row.

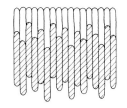

Fig.3 *The second row completed.*

4   When the second row is complete, work a third row varying the length of all your stitches slightly to give a soft look to your shading (see Fig. 4).

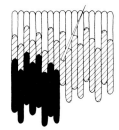

Fig.4 *Vary the length of your stitches to give your shading a soft look.*

5   Change the colours as the work progresses. Remember that while the work is progressing some of the length of the stitch is lost as subsequent rows are worked, so it may be necessary to work several rows of some shades to achieve the required effect.

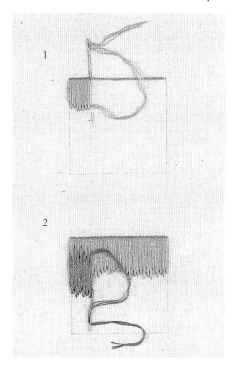

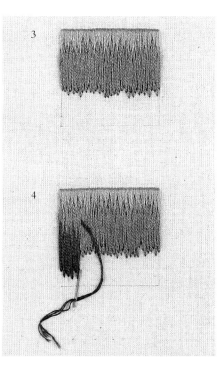

Directional Long and Short Stitch

As with tapestry shading, directional long and short stitch is worked over a split stitch edge but instead of the stitches being vertical they take the direction of the growth of the object being worked.

1   Occasionally it may be necessary to add an extra small stitch to swing the angle of the stitches round. Always come up in the shape and go down over the split stitch edge (see Fig. 5).

Fig.5 *Always bring your needle up in the shape and go down over the split stitch edge.*

2   In the second row, come up in the ends of the stitches and split them working a row of stitches in the long and short stitches of the first row. These

should vary very slightly in length to give a soft change of colour (see Fig. 6). If you find this difficult at first, lengthen the short stitches then the long ones until you feel confident.

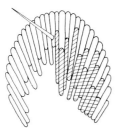

Fig.6 *Vary the length of your stitches slightly.*

3   The third row of stitches is worked as for the second row (see Fig. 7). Note that after the first row of long and short stitches all the stitches are of a similar length to the long ones in the first row, varied just a little to give a softer look.

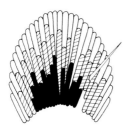

Fig.7 *Work the third row in the same way as the second.*

4   Fig. 8 shows how to work a simple flower shape and the order of working. A split stitch edge should be worked against every previously worked petal. It would probably be helpful to make a shaded drawing of the subject to be worked in pencil or water-soluble crayons.

Fig.8 *The order of working a simple flower shape.*

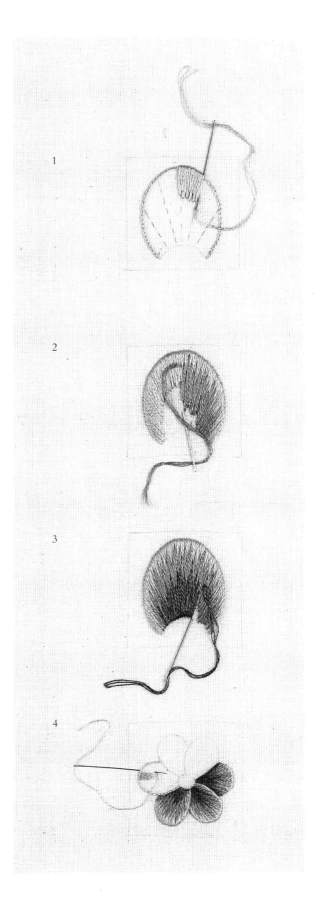

EXERCISE FOR BEGINNERS

As a first exercise in each section a simple design is drawn from an antique Majolica tile. The uncomplicated shapes are adaptable for each technique, and can be repeated to make a larger piece of work varying both colour and stitches. The shapes of the design should help you to understand long and short without too much difficulty. This piece includes satin stitch, tapestry shading and long and short directional shading, and is worked in four shades of gold-coloured stranded cotton.

Materials

- Background is cream dupion mounted on to a preshrunk cotton with herringbone stitch. Match the grain of both fabrics. This should be large enough to fit a 25 cm (10 inch) ring frame
- A 25 cm (10 inch) ring frame that fits a floorstand, table clamp or seat frame. This will enable you to work with two hands
- A range of four gold stranded cottons, such as 301, 302, 314, 324
- Crewel needles nos. 8-10, the finest you can use

Preparation

1 Use a light box to transfer the design on to the background (see page 15).
2 Paint the lines with a very fine line or use a hard pencil.
3 Mount the background into a ring frame very tightly.

Instructions

1 Corner sections are worked in slanting satin stitch. Work inside the shape first, the stitches are worked over split stitch on the slant. When the inside shape is completed, work split against satin and, on the top edge, work over in slanting satin in the opposite direction to the first row. To secure the long satin stitches, couch with a matching thread through the centre of the shapes. Colours used 324 and 314.

2 Work the centre in tapestry shaded long and short stitch, working a split stitch round the shape first. Start on one edge with shade 314 and work straight across with a change of shade to 324 in the centre, and back to 314 to finish the shape (see page 27).

3 The four petal shapes are worked in long and short shading, with a direction which takes the lines of a growing petal shape. First split stitch the outside edge of the shape. Start shading with a long and short row of stitches round the tips in the pale shade 301. This will give the staggering needed. After the first row all the stitches are a similar length. Bring the needle up inside the shape and go down over the split stitch to give a good edge. Continue working down the shape, changing the colours to 302 and 314. Bring the needle up in the ends of the previous stitches in subsequent rows. When learning it may be helpful to work into the short stitches first, then work a row coming up in the ends of the long stitches. When this is mastered, try working both long and short stitches together, and stagger the length of the stitches to give a random look to your work (see page 25, Fig. 7). Remember to keep your stitches a good length throughout; if the stitches become too small the work can look rather rough.

4 From the centre points, work stem stitch lines changing shades from 314 to 302, to 301 at the top.

STITCH DIAGRAM

This small exercise is worked in four shades of Anchor stranded cotton: 301, 302, 314, 324. Use two strands throughout.

1 *Work satin stitch over split stitch edge (324, 314), direction is shown on diagram.*

2 *Tapestry shading in centre (314, 324).*

3 *Natural directional shading, direction is shown on diagram.*

4 *Stem stitch line (301, 302, 314).*

5 *Couch down centre of satin with four strands of matching thread.*

LANDSCAPE

This project is worked without stitch direction using the tapestry shading method. This is a helpful way to learn long and short shading without the worry of the direction of the stitch. As the name suggests, this type of shading has the appearance of the shading of a woven tapestry, with the stitches being worked straight down the project.

We have chosen a sunset with trees silhouetted against it. You probably have photographs you have taken of similar beautiful skies which could be used to produce your own project. Our design is of Beaver Hills, Canada, and is worked in one strand of 14 shades of Anchor stranded cotton with the trees worked in stem stitch, using black Anchor stranded and DMC black machine thread. The colour plan for the change of shades is on page 30.

Materials

- A square peg frame dressed with a firm preshrunk calico (see page 10)
- Fabric the size of the project plus allowance for mounting
- Crewel needles nos. 9 or 10
- Anchor stranded cotton threads nos. 381, 45, 43, 20, 19, 13, 11, 10, 324, 314, 303, 302, 301 and 403
- DMC black machine thread no. 310 size 50

Preparation

1 Draw your design on to good quality tracing paper.
2 Prick and pounce the design on to the background fabric (see page 13).
3 Paint the design of the tree trunks and thick branches only with fine lines.

Instructions

1 The tapestry shaded sky is worked from the top and worked down changing shades as you go, leaving a gap for the tree trunk.
2 The fine branches are worked on top of the tapestry shaded sky as work progresses or when the sky is complete in the fine DMC machine thread.
3 The trunks of the trees are worked in rows of stem stitch using black stranded cotton (see page 29).

Landscape, partly worked by Tracy Franklin.

The sky is worked first, followed by the tree trunks.

Finally small twigs and branches are added.

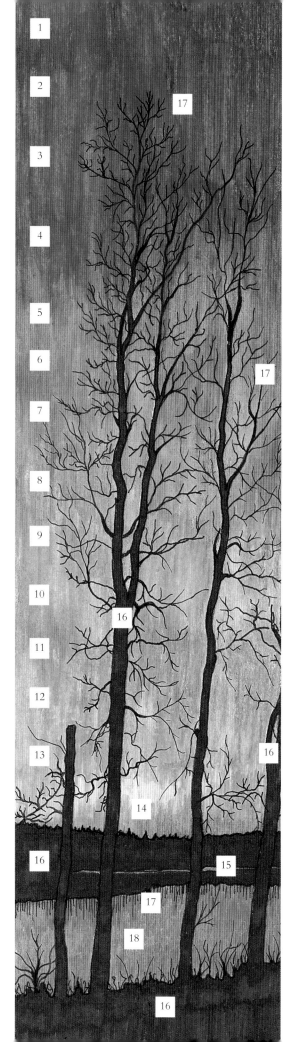

STITCH DIAGRAM

1 *Anchor 381*

2 *Anchor 45*

3 *Anchor 43*

4 *Anchor 20*

5 *Anchor 19*

6 *Anchor 13*

7 *Anchor 11*

8 *Anchor 10*

9 *Anchor 324*

10 *Anchor 314*

11 *Anchor 303*

12 *Anchor 302*

13 *Anchor 301*

14 *Anchor 302, 303, 314, 324*

15 *Anchor 13, 11, 10, 324*

16 *Anchor 403*

17 *DMC machine thread size 50, no. 310*

18 *Anchor 13, 11, 10, 324, 314*

IRIS

There is nothing that will give an embroiderer more pleasure than to work a silk shaded flower. To start with, choose a well drawn flower with a not too complicated structure. Make a shading of your flower on paper. The stranded cottons should be well graded in tonal values.

Materials

- A square peg frame mounted with preshrunk calico (see page 10)
- A square of slub silk the size of the project plus mounting allowance
- Crewel needles nos. 8, 9 or 10
- Anchor stranded cotton threads: greens 264, 265, 266, 267, 268 and 269, the darkest; yellows 305, 306, 307, 308 and 309, the darkest; pinks 892, 893, 894, 895, 896 and 897, the darkest

Preparation

1 Mount the slub silk background on to the dressed square frame (see page 10).
2 Trace the design on to good quality tracing paper and prick the design, then pounce and paint the design on to the mounted background fabric with a very fine line (see page 13).
3 With a thread colour matching the background silk, stab stitch round the design on the inside edge of the paint line in one strand.

Instructions

A split stitch in two strands is worked round the shapes first in the colour of the long and short to be worked over the split stitch. The long and short is also worked in two strands throughout.

1 Always work underneath shapes first. First work the leaf at the back in 264, 265, 266, 267 and 268. When the leaf is completed, work vein lines on top of the long and short in one strand of 269 in stem stitch.
2 Work the small back shape in gold no. 309 and 308; split stitch the outside edge first.
3 For the underneath area, use gold no. 309; no split stitch needed.

Iris worked by Debra Barrett.

4   For the left-hand top back petal, split stitch round outside edge in a pale shade and work over in long and short stitch in nos. 893, 894, 895, 896 and 897.

5   Split stitch all round the small turnover on the last petal then work long and short stitch from the inside edge to the outside in nos. 892 and 893.

6   Work the small section of a back petal with split stitch on the small bottom edge. Long and short stitch in nos. 896 and 897.

7   Split stitch the right-hand bottom petal along the bottom edge; work in long and short shading from the edge in light to dark in the shadows using nos. 893, 894, 895, 896 and 897.

8   Now work the bottom left petal. Split stitch against the previously worked leaf and round the edge, in a medium pale shade and work long and short as no. 7 in nos. 892, 893, 894, 895 and 896.

9   Work split stitch on the edge against no. 7. Then work long and short from the outside, medium pink to dark at the base using shade nos. 893, 894, 895, 896 and 897.

10 This petal is outlined in split stitch round the top edge and down the right-hand side using a mid-pink shade. The long and short stitch is worked from the edge into the centre of the flower. The shading produces a wavy edge. As you will be working with a range of shades, it will be helpful to have needles threaded with each shade in use. The shades are nos. 893, 894, 895, 896 and 897.

11 The three top calyx leaves are first split stitched against no. 6 and no. 9 in shade nos. 265, 266, 267 and 268.

12 The turned-over edge of the bottom right petal can be now worked in nos. 892, 893, 894, 895, 896 and 897. Work split stitch against the previous work, round the edge of the turnover.

13 Now work the centre petal: stitch split stitch round the edge and against the previous work and long and short in shade nos. 892, 893, 894, 895 and 896.

14 Split stitch round the two stamens. Work in long and short in gold nos. 305, 306 and 308.

15 Work the lower stamen in French knots in three strands of Anchor stranded in gold nos. 305, 306, 307

and 308; shade from light to dark.

16, 17 and 18 Now carry out the calyx work in order, working a split stitch against all previous work. Work in long and short in greens nos. 264, 265, 266, 267 and 268.

19 Work split stitch all round the stem, then work long and short stitch in greens nos. 266, 267, 268 and 269. Add the vein lines to the finished stem in one strand of no. 269 in stem stitch.

20 For the right-hand leaf lower section, work the round edge and against previous work with stem stitch. Work in long and short in greens nos. 264, 265, 266 and 267, working from light at the base to dark at the turnover. Add vein lines in one strand of no. 269.

21 For the turnover, split stitch round the shape and work in long and short in green nos. 264, 265 and 266. Add vein lines in one strand of no. 269.

STITCH DIAGRAM

1 Back leaf worked in green 264, 265, 266, 267, 268, vein lines worked in 269

2 Gold 309, 308

3 Gold 309

4 Left-hand top petal pink 893, 894, 895, 896, 897

5 Small turn over of no. 4 petal pale pink 892, 893

6 Back petal worked in dark pink 896, 897

7 Right-hand bottom petal in 893, 894, 895, 896, 897

8 Bottom left petal pink 892, 893, 894, 895, 896

9 Pink in shades as 7

10 Top right hand petal 893, 894, 895, 896, 897

11 Top green calyx leaves 265, 266, 267, 268

12 Turned over petal edge pink 892, 893, 894, 895, 896, 897

13 Centre petal pink 892, 893, 894, 895, 896

14 Top two stamens yellow 305, 306, 308

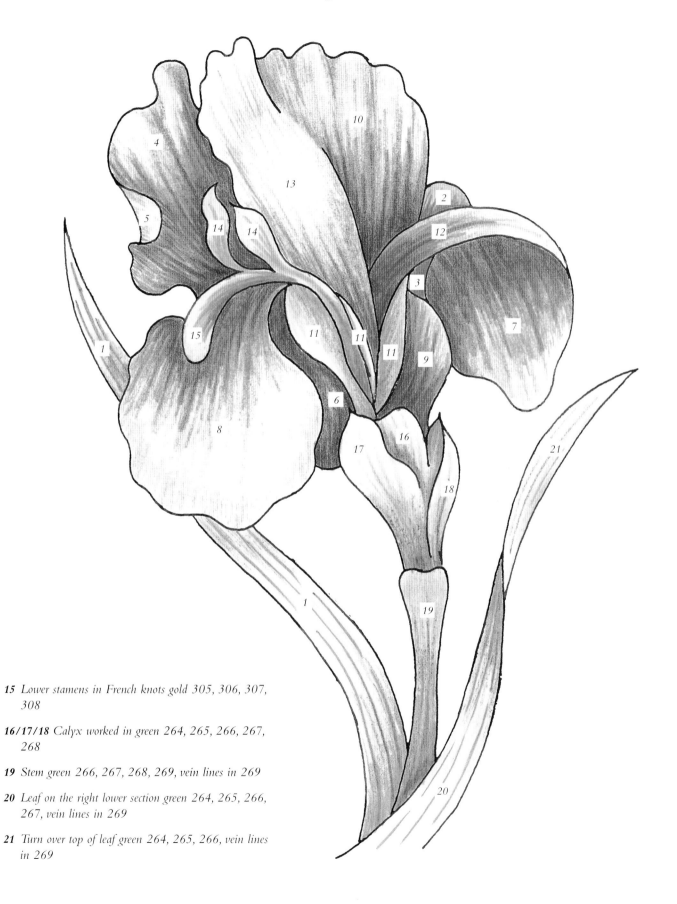

15 Lower stamens in French knots gold *305, 306, 307, 308*

16/17/18 Calyx worked in green *264, 265, 266, 267, 268*

19 Stem green *266, 267, 268, 269, vein lines in 269*

20 Leaf on the right lower section green *264, 265, 266, 267, vein lines in 269*

21 Turn over top of leaf green *264, 265, 266, vein lines in 269*

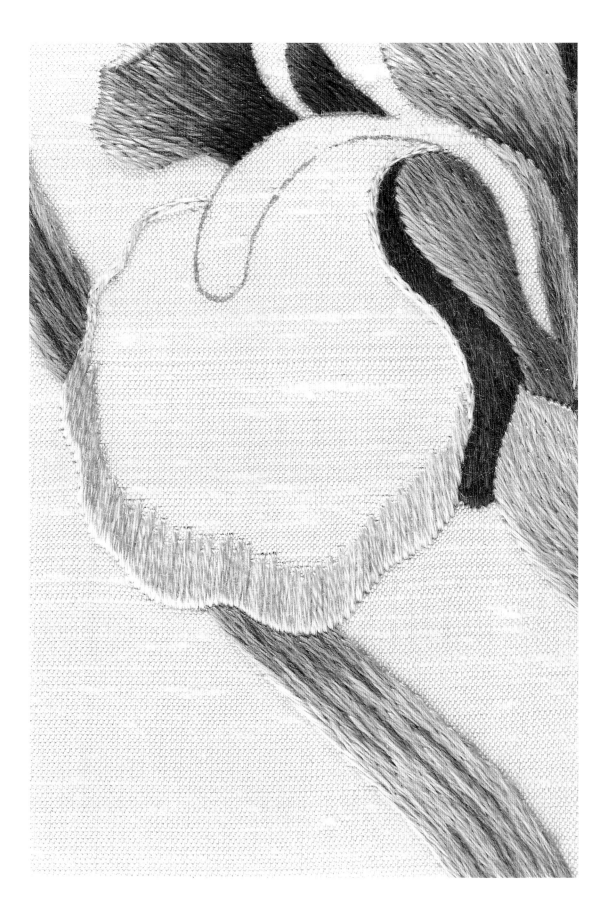

DOG PORTRAIT

One of the most delightful ways of using silk shading is to embroider an animal. The animals worked by apprentices at the Royal School always intrigue the public and many visitors want to know how they are worked. We hope this project will help.

Choose a design that is not too complicated. Take photographs of your subject from different angles to give you ideas for the least complicated design angle. Your design should be large enough to work in the various shades needed to bring the animal to life. Threads should be selected with great care to give the whole range of colours included in the coat of the animal. Dexter, a Golden Labrador, needs 17 shades to bring out the various tones in his coat.

Materials

- A square peg frame
- Preshrunk cotton for backing the silk
- Background fabric the size of the project plus allowance for mounting
- Crewel needles nos. 9 or 10
- Anchor stranded threads nos. 381, 380, 358, 374, 943, 372, 403, 401, 848, 393, 392, 830, 390 and 926
- DMC stranded threads nos. 839, 435 and 3787
- Gütermann invisible thread col. 854

Preparation

1 Dye the silk background with silk dyes in a diffuser. In this one we have sprayed more heavily at the top.
2 Dress a square peg frame with preshrunk cotton and mount with the dyed background fabric (see page 10).
3 Tack a centre line both ways. Tighten the frame.
4 Trace your design on to good quality (60 gsm) tracing paper with the centre lines marked. Prick the design (see page 13).
5 Lining up the centre lines, pounce the design on to background then paint the design with a very fine line (see page 14).

6 Stab stitch with a fine thread that matches the background along the paint lines to prevent the fabric puckering.
7 Refer to stage and colour plan. Split stitch on the outside edges and against previous work.

Instructions

1 Leg, Anchor nos. 393, 392, 830, 390 and 926.
2 Paw on the left, Anchor nos. 393, 392, 381, 380, 390, 830, 372 and 926.
3 Claws on the left, Anchor no. 358, DMC no. 839 and Anchor nos. 381 and 392.
4 Toes on the left, Anchor nos. 393, 392, 926, 381 and 380.
5 Leg on the left, DMC no. 3787, Anchor nos. 393, 392 and 372.
6 Leg on the left, Anchor nos. 393, 392, 390, 830, 926 and 372.
7 Leg on the right, DMC nos. 3787 and 839, Anchor nos. 380 and 393.
8 Claws on the right, Anchor nos. 358, 381 and 392, DMC no. 839.
9 Leg on the right and paw, Anchor nos. 372, 393, 830, 392, 926, 390 and DMC no. 3787.

Dog worked by Tracy Franklin.

10 Top of leg on right, DMC no. 3787, Anchor nos. 393, 392 and 830.

11 Back on right, DMC nos. 3787 and 435, Anchor nos. 392, 830, 372, 393, 943 and 380.

12 Back on right, Anchor nos. 926, 390, 830, 392, 372 and 393.

13 Back, DMC nos. 839 and 3787, Anchor nos. 393, 392, 830, 372, 374 and 943.

14 Neck, DMC nos. 3787 and 839, Anchor nos. 393, 392, 943 and 374.

15 Neck, DMC nos. 839, 435 and 3787 and Anchor no. 943.

16 Head, DMC nos. 435, 3787 and 839, Anchor nos. 943, 374, 393, 392 and 372.

17 Head, DMC no. 3787, Anchor nos. 374, 943, 372, 393 and 392.

18 Head, Anchor nos. 390, 830, 392 and 372.

19 Head, Anchor nos. 943, 393, 392 and 372.

20 Eyes: pupil, Anchor nos. 403 and 381; iris, Anchor nos. 943 and 403; highlight, Anchor no. 393.

21 Under eye, Anchor nos. 381 and 403; highlight, Anchor no. 393.

22 Dark area under eye, Anchor nos. 403 and 381.

23 Eyelid, Anchor nos. 403 and 358.

24 Forehead, Anchor nos. 390, 392, 372, 393, 830, 926, 943 and 374.

25 Eyebrows, DMC no. 3787, Anchor nos. 380, 390, 392, 372, 393, 830, 926, 943 and 374.

26 Under the eyes, Anchor nos. 830, 390, 926, 393, 392 and 372.

27 Cheek, Anchor nos. 374, 943, 393, 372, 392 and 830.

28 Nose, Anchor nos. 374, 943, 372, 390, 392 and 393.

29 Nose, dark shades, DMC nos. 839 and 3787, Anchor no. 374; light shades, Anchor nos. 372, 392, 393 and 943.

(Continued on page 42.)

STITCH DIAGRAM

*Refer to main instructions
for detail of stitching
stages 1–40.*

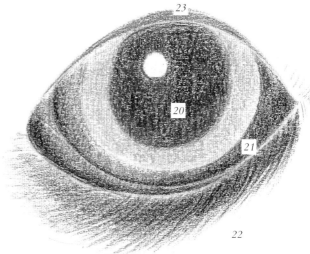

Dog Portrait

8 Toenails

40 Whiskers

3 Toenails

41

30 Cheeks, Anchor nos. 392, 372, 380 and 390; dark area, DMC no. 3787.

31 Above nose, Anchor no. 403; around nose, Anchor no. 848.

32 Mouth, Anchor nos. 392, 830, 390, 401 and 848.

33 Nose, worked in tapestry shading, Anchor nos. 403, 393 and 381, DMC no. 839.

34 Ear on the right, Anchor nos. 358, 374, 392 and 372, DMC no. 435; dark areas, DMC no. 3787 and Anchor nos. 393 and 380.

35 Top of ear tufts, Anchor nos. 393, 392 and 830.

36 Ear on the left, Anchor nos. 830, 392, 943, 374 and 372, DMC no. 435; dark areas, DMC nos. 3787 and 839, Anchor nos. 393, 358 and 380.

37 Edge of ear on the left, DMC no. 435, Anchor nos. 943, 374, 358 and 392; dark areas, Anchor no. 380 and DMC no. 839.

38 Tip of ear on the left, Anchor nos. 943, 374, 358, 393 and 392, DMC no. 435; dark areas, Anchor no. 380, DMC nos. 839 and 3787.

39 Tuft on ear on the left, Anchor no. 926.

40 Whiskers, worked in invisible thread col. 854 Gütermann U81 skala.

TREE BARK

The inspiration for this design came from a study of tree bark. It is always tempting to make a design from a complete subject, but some of the most interesting pieces of work are arrived at by taking a section of natural materials, and exploring the textures and colours and then translating your sketches and source material into fabric and thread. Add to the work anything that can be stitched to give the desired effect. Fabric paints and texture gels could come into their own for this type of project and could be used in conjunction with the long and short shading. In this tree bark design we have sponge dyed our background fabric.

Materials

- A square peg frame mounted with preshrunk calico
- Color Fun dyes in black, brown and bronze
- A square of good quality felt for padding
- Crewel needles in a selection of sizes
- Any interesting threads could be used. We have used Anchor stranded cotton nos. 380, 381, 382, 403, 360, 801, 433 and 365; Appletons crewel wool nos. 588, 585, 584 and 582; Anchor soft embroidery no. 369; Sirdar no. 114; DMC perle no. 8 - 433, 434 and 781; Anchor perle no. 8 - 375; DMC perle no. 5 - 610, 829 and 780; Anchor perle no. 5 - 907; Jaeger Grace in brown; chenille, ribbon and lambswool in similar shades

Preparation

1 Sponge dye the background fabric with Color Fun dyes then leave to dry.

2 Pounce and paint the design on to the background.

3 Pounce the design on to the felt and cut out using 1-4 layers (see page 13).

4 Work underneath areas of the design first.

5 Use long and short stitch and some couching throughout. Work split stitch to raise one edge over another. Refer to the stitch plan.

Instructions

1-4 Pad with layers of felt in the areas selected.

5 Anchor stranded cotton no. 403.

6 Anchor stranded cotton nos. 403 and 588.

7 Anchor stranded cotton no. 382.

8 Anchor stranded cotton nos. 403 and 382.

9 Anchor stranded cotton nos. 380, 381 and 382.

10 DMC perle 8-433, Anchor perle 8-375.

11 Anchor stranded cotton nos. 403 and 382, Appletons crewel wool nos. 588 and 584.

12 Appletons crewel wool nos. 588, 584, 582.

13 Appletons crewel wool no. 584.

14 Anchor stranded cotton nos. 380, 381 and 382.

15 Appletons crewel wool nos. 584 and 582.

16 Appletons crewel wool nos. 582, 584 and 588.

17 Appletons crewel wool nos. 584 and 582, Anchor stranded cotton nos. 381 and 380.

18 Anchor stranded cotton nos. 403, Appletons crewel wool nos. 588 and 585.

19 DMC perle 5-610, Appletons crewel wool no. 582.

20 Anchor stranded cotton nos. 381 and 360, DMC stranded cotton no. 839.

21 Anchor stranded cotton nos. 382, 380 and 801, Anchor perle 8-434 and perle 5-780.

22 Anchor stranded cotton nos. 801 and 433.

Tree Bark worked by Melissa Cheeseman.

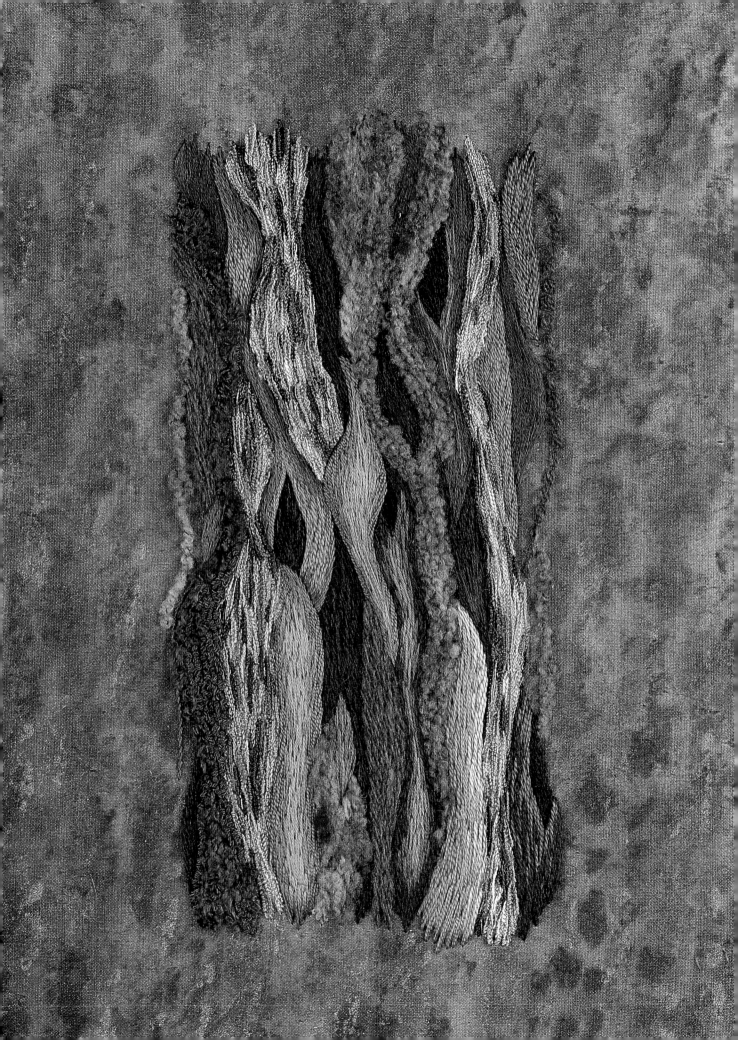

23 Anchor stranded cotton no. 801.

24 Anchor perle 5-907, DMC perle 8-434 and 781.

25 Appletons crewel wool no. 582, Anchor stranded cotton no. 579, Anchor soft embroidery no. 369.

26 Anchor perle 8-375, Anchor stranded cotton nos. 433 and 365.

27 Lambswool mixture.

28 Jaeger Grace.

29 Ribbon from chenille wool.

30 Chenille Sirdar no. 114, couched.

31 Anchor perle 8-375, Anchor stranded cotton nos. 365 and 433.

32 Chenille, Sirdar no. 114.

33 DMC perle 5-610 and 829.

34 Chenille, Sirdar no. 114, couched.

35 Lambswool, couched.

36 Anchor stranded cotton no. 801, stem stitch.

STITCH DIAGRAM

1 *One layer of felt*

2 *Two layers of felt*

3 *Three layers of felt*

4 *Four layers of felt*

5 *Anchor 403*

6 *Anchor 403*

7 *Anchor 382*

8 *Anchor 403, 382*

9 *Anchor 380, 381, 382*

10 *DMC Perle 8-435, Anchor Perle 8-375*

11 *Anchor 403, 382, Appleton 588, 584*

12 *Appleton 588, 584, 582*

13 *Appleton 584*

14 *Anchor 380, 381, 382*

15 *Appleton 584, 582*

16 *Appleton 582, 584, 588*

17 *Appleton 584, 582, Anchor 381, 380*

18 *Anchor 403, Appleton 588, 585*

19 *DMC Perle 5-610, Appleton 582*

20 *Anchor 381, 360*

21 *Anchor 382, 380, 801, Anchor Perle 8-434, Anchor Perle 5-780*

22 *Anchor 801, 433*

23 *Anchor 801*

24 *Anchor Perle 5-907, DMC Perle 8-434, 781*

25 *Appleton 582, Anchor 579, Anchor soft cotton 369*

26 *Anchor Perle 8-375, Anchor 433, 365*

27 *Lambswool mixtures*

28 *Jaegar grace*

29 *Ribbon*

30 *Chenille (couched)*

31 *Anchor Perle 8-375, Anchor 365, 433*

32 *Chenille (couched)*

33 *DMC Perle 5-610, 829*

34 *Chenille (couched)*

35 *Lambswool (couched)*

36 *Anchor 801 (stem stitch)*

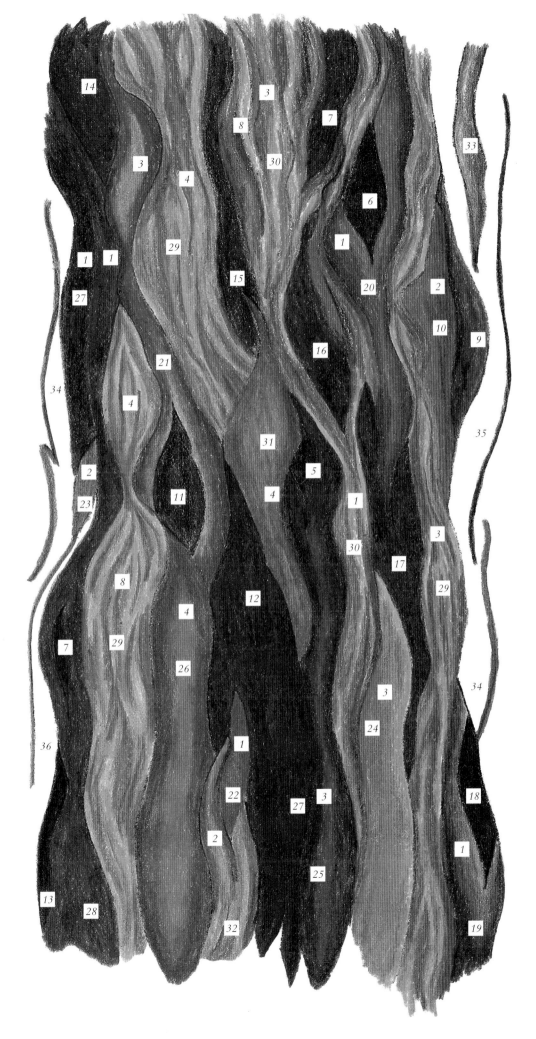

INTRODUCING CREWEL WORK

The origins of crewel work would probably be found in the cottages and dwellings of the earliest spinners. The two-ply wool they spun would almost certainly have been used to decorate their clothing, if only with simple stitches like cross stitch, chain stitch and herringbone. Sadly very early examples have not survived. The first real example of crewel embroidery in existence is the Bayeux Tapestry. This 900-year-old piece of work is in fact a piece of crewel embroidery, not a woven tapestry as the name implies. This embroidery is a wonderful account of the Norman Conquest and a very detailed record of the social history of the time. The 70.35 m (231-foot) long embroidery was worked in just eight shades of crewel wool. The majority of the design was worked in a laid stitch, where the threads are stitched across the shapes from side to side with just a tiny stitch on the back of the work. These laid stitches were then held in place by regularly couched threads and neatened with stem stitch.

After the working of the Bayeux Tapestry, no crewel embroidery survived for 600 years. Henry VIII plundered the monasteries and abbeys and as a result the wonderful church embroidery of the *Opus Anglicanum* period was no longer made and much of the existing work was destroyed or cut up for domestic use. The wealth of the sixteenth and early seventeenth century was used to build very grand houses and this increased the demand for furnishing textiles. Embroidery was now found on wall and bed hangings, cushions, upholstery, table carpets and beautiful costumes, and a great deal was decorated with crewel embroidery.

At this time the fortune-seeking merchants of the East India Company brought back to England brilliant coloured textiles. These were often the tree of life designs, incorporating exotic birds and animals. This formed the basis for the Jacobean designs we know so well. The early monochromatic Jacobean embroideries were worked in just a few stitches – a lot of stem stitch, back stitch and chain stitch with seeding. These little seeding stitches were as wide as they were long, and were repeated all over shapes, used very densely to produce shadow and more spaced out to give highlighted design areas. As more dyes became available, the colours of the Jacobean embroideries began to imitate the colours of the imported Eastern textiles.

Designs included wonderful birds and other creatures, and these were embroidered with an amazing range of stitches. The bodies were worked in brick stitch, burden stitch, and shaded long and short stitch; the tails, wings and stripes were worked in block shading and satin stitch, and rows of beautifully shaded stem stitch and chain stitch; heads, feet and claws were worked in stitches like French knots and bullion knots.

The huge Jacobean leaf shapes were cut up into interesting areas and these were decorated with square filling stitches which gave a lacy effect when used against the heavier long and short stitch. The edges of the designs were decorated with fly stitches, sword stitch and rows of little running stitches, all adding interest to the bold shapes of the design.

Towards the end of the seventeenth century crewel work designs were not so much an all-over pattern as the early designs, but more a collection of motifs, worked in a lighter style, reducing the enormous rows of hillocks found at the base of early Jacobean designs to small decorative strips. A very good example of this is the Abigail Pett embroidery in the Victoria and Albert

A detail of a Jacobean embroidery showing the use of seeding stitches to give the subject depth, seventeenth century, RSN Collection.

Museum. This style of embroidery provides real inspiration, and is probably responsible for keeping Jacobean crewel work alive and popular even to the present day. The designs now become finer and were influenced by more naturalistic plants and flowers, many of English origin. This change of design by the eighteenth century produced more delicate work than the enormous early Jacobean hangings and at the same time reduced the variety of stitches used.

The eighteenth century saw a different use of crewel embroidery. There was a general revival of interest in paintings and with this came the embroidery skill known as needlepainting. This was the reproduction of portraits in crewel wool, in mostly long and short stitch or split stitch. The skill needed to carry out this work was such that only a few needlewomen achieved a high standard. Some used painted detail on areas like the faces. Most embroiderers were happy to return to the less difficult embroidery using flowers and leaves stitched in silk or crewel wool.

In the mid-nineteenth century, crewel work was again popular. William Morris and Edward Burne-Jones found it suited the flowing nature of their designs. Long and short stitch could be made to flow with the growth of leaves and flowers. It also moulded the faces and hands of figures. In 1872 the Royal School of Needlework was founded and with the collaboration of William Morris, a designer at the School and his daughter Mary, who taught there, crewel embroidery continued to be carried out to very high standards and probably contributed to the School's success when competing with the industrial sewing machine.

A detail of a Jacobean
embroidery showing animals
on traditional hillocks,
seventeenth century, RSN
Collection.

Crewel work has continued to be part of the training of a Royal School embroiderer. With the knowledge and skill of the techniques and stitches comes the confidence to adapt what has been learnt to other types of embroidery. Burden stitch, seeding and crossbar fillings can be adapted to goldwork. Satin stitch, bullion knots and raised stem band are wonderful on whitework. Many stitches find their origins in crewel work and it is therefore in any embroiderer's interest to study it well and to practise at least some of the stitches and techniques used. Yes, this is a very old, traditional technique but it can be updated beautifully and gives a great deal of pleasure.

Crewel work was originally worked in the seventeenth and eighteenth centuries on a linen and cotton twill weave fabric. This was hard wearing and easy to stitch on and can still be obtained today. Twill is a wonderful firm fabric to stitch on, but is rather expensive. Other fabrics that are firmly woven can be used. For example, cotton satin works well and can also be dyed for modern treatments of crewel work.

APPROACH TO CREWEL WORK

Fine crewel wool is used for the embroidery. This comes in a large range of colours and will give plenty of variety. The thick tapestry wools are not suitable and would make the work too bulky.

The selection of needles is quite important. The needle should take the crewel wool easily through the eye without damaging the thread. If the thread keeps breaking the eye may be too small and if it is difficult to stitch accurately, the needle may be too large. Most people like using a chenille needle as these have long eyes and sharp points, but crewel needles, as the name suggests, are also suitable.

The choice of frame will be a square peg frame, as this can be kept drum tight and thus avoids unsightly puckers (see page 10). To practise on, or for small designs, a deep-sided ring frame would be suitable if the fabric is kept very taut.

To choose a design you need to decide if you want to be traditional or take a more modern approach. The worked examples in this book will give you some ideas. An infinite source of designs could come from studying old embroideries and textiles in museums and old houses. Take a sketchbook and draw some small areas of old embroideries that interest you. Choose an interesting leaf shape and an animal or bird, draw several of these and pick out the areas you like best, blow your drawings up on a photocopier and then arrange them on a piece of paper to give a pleasing effect. Cut a window mount out of paper and set this over your design until you find an area you like. Trace this arrangement on to tracing paper and prick and pounce the design on to your fabric, then paint the design (see pages 14 and 15).

Before commencing the embroidery, it is a good idea to make a stitch plan of where your stitches are going to be placed on your design (see Jacobean leaf sampler, page 60).

After a study of a Jacobean embroidery at the Victoria & Albert Museum, this piece was worked by a First Year Apprentice, Jenny Addin, 1996. Over twenty stitches and fillings are used – note the little stitches decorating the edges of the shapes.

EXERCISE FOR BEGINNERS

This exercise uses the Majolica tile again to enable you to practise on a small piece before embarking on a larger project.

Materials

- The background is a fine closely woven linen large enough to fit on to a 25 cm (10-inch) ring frame, 2.5 cm (1 inch) deep
- A range of shades of Appletons crewel wool nos. 472, 474, 475 and 476
- An accurately drawn and inked design with the centre marked both ways
- Crewel needles no. 8 or 9

Preparation

1 Tack the centre of the background fabric both ways.
2 To transfer the design on to the fabric we have used a light box. Place the inked design on the light box and place the fabric on the top, matching up the design centre lines and the fabric tack lines. Switch on the light and trace the design on to the fabric with a sharp, hard pencil (2H) or use a fine paintbrush and paint (see page 15).
3 Mount the design into a ring frame, making sure it is as tight as possible to avoid puckering and poor stitch tension.

Instructions

Nine different stitches are included in this crewel work piece and you will find them all in the Stitch Glossary (see page 144).

1 French knots, using two threads in the needle, worked in Appletons crewel wool nos. 475 and 476.
2 Bullion knots, using one thread, worked in Appletons crewel wool nos. 475 and 476.
3 Buttonhole stitch, using one thread each of Appletons crewel wool nos. 472 and 474 in the needle.
4 Raised stem band, using one thread, worked in Appletons crewel wool nos. 472 and 474.
5 Square filling work crossbar worked in Appletons crewel wool no. 476, using one strand and tied down with small stitches in Appletons crewel wool no. 476. Decorative crosses: large in one strand of Appletons crewel wool no. 475 and small crosses in one strand of Appletons crewel wool no. 472.
6 Block shading centre over split stitch worked in two strands of Appletons crewel wool nos. 472, 474 and 475.
7 Laidwork is worked in Appletons crewel wool nos. 476, 475 and 474 using one strand with crossbar filling on the top in one strand Appletons crewel wool no. 472.
8 Stem stitch outside edge of petal shapes in one strand Appletons crewel wool no. 472.
9 Chain stitch from the corners of block shading centre in one strand of Appletons crewel wool no. 472. Work outside petal shapes.

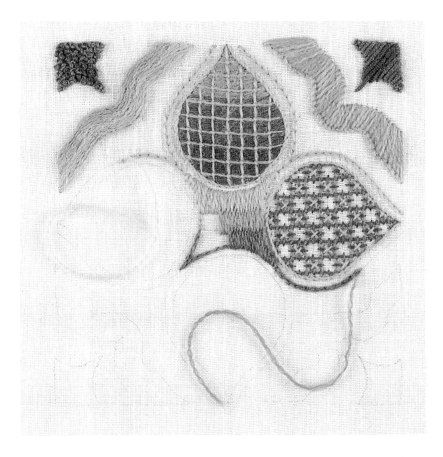

STITCH DIAGRAM

This exercise is worked in Appleton Wool

1 *French knots, 2 threads in shades 475, 476*

2 *Bullion knots, 1 thread in shades 475, 476*

3 *Buttonhole closed, 2 threads mixed in the needle 472, 474*

4 *Raised stem band, 2 threads in shades 472, 474*

5 *Square filling, cross bar in 476, crosses in 472, 475*

6 *Block shading, 2 threads 472, 474, 475*

7 *Laidwork, 1 thread in 476, 475, 474, outline stem stitch 472*

8 *Outline petals in stem stitch, 1 thread 472*

9 *Chain stitch in 1 thread 472*

JACOBEAN LEAF SAMPLER

To learn a lovely variety of stitches, there is no better place to start than a piece of Jacobean embroidery. Quite a surprising number of stitches can be included in a design like this small Jacobean leaf motif, which uses crewel wool on linen twill.

If you want to produce your own design, research old embroideries for inspiration. Large Jacobean leaf shapes can be divided up easily to include a variety of stitches. Crossbar fillings give a nice lacy look when worked against the heavier techniques like block shading and long and short. Use stitches like bullion knots, French knots and seeding to provide interesting texture to a design. Make a copy of your design and plan out your stitches before commencing work. This forward planning will help you produce a good finish.

Using twill as a background fabric, your colours will be quite unrestricted and the firmness of the fabric will help the finish of your work. When working a small design, choose two complementary ranges of crewel wool, balancing the use of colours throughout the design.

Materials

- A piece of linen twill or firm fabric the size of the finished project plus 10 cm (4 inches) for mounting No backing is needed
- Crewel needles nos. 6–9
- Your design drawn on to good quality (60 gsm) tracing paper, with the centre marked
- A square peg frame (see page 10) or a deep-sided ring frame
- One skein each Appletons crewel wool nos. 901, 902, 903, 904, 905, 291, 292, 293, 295, 296 and 298

Preparation

1 If you are using twill, the grain should run across the work from the bottom left-hand corner to the top right.

2 Dress the square peg frame, marking centre lines (see page 10).

3 Prick and pounce the design on to the background fabric and paint the design with a fine line (see page 13).

Instructions

Use a single thread throughout. Work the underneath sections of the design first. Refer to the plan.

1 In this section work the grouped buttonhole, shading the colours working light at the top down to dark at the base, using Appletons crewel wool nos. 292, 293, 295, 296 and 298.

2 The main stem is worked in block shading in stripes of three shades, Appletons crewel wool nos. 903, 904 and 905.

3 The tendril is worked in rows of shaded stem stitch, using Appletons crewel wool nos. 292, 293 and 295.

4 Work a split stitch round the edge of this leaf and then work long and short with five shades of wool, Appletons crewel wool nos. 292, 293, 295, 296 and 298.

5 The top group of small leaves is worked in block shading, working from the top to the bottom leaf.

Jacobean Leaf Sampler worked by Jennifer Malone.

Work over a split stitch, which is worked against the previous leaf, using Appletons crewel wool nos. 291, 292, 293, 903, 904 and 905.

6 The small central top leaf is worked over a previously worked split stitch edge in four shades, Appletons crewel wool nos. 292, 293, 904 and 905.

7 The top left- and right-hand side leaves have central shapes worked in chequered filling using Appletons crewel wool nos. 292, 293, 902 and 903.

8 This is outlined in coral stitch using Appletons crewel wool no. 904.

9 The outside edge is worked in heavy chain stitch using Appletons crewel wool no. 295.

10 The central small leaflets are worked in bullion knots using Appletons crewel wool no. 295.

11 Either side of the bullion knot leaflets, work the leaves in satin stitch using Appletons crewel wool no. 295.

12 The stem is worked in coral stitch using Appletons crewel wool no. 296.

13 The outline is worked in a row of detached chain stitches in Appletons crewel wool no. 293 which are whipped with no. 902.

14 The bottom left-hand leaf is worked in Cretan stitch using Appletons crewel wool no. 904.

15 The bottom right-hand leaf is worked in Vandyke stitch using Appletons crewel wool no. 904.

16 Work rows of shaded chain stitch on the outer edge of nos. 14 and 15 leaves, working from the dark edge to the light centre, using Appletons crewel wool nos. 292, 293, 295 and 296.

17 This left-hand large leaf is worked in a crossbar filling. Basic trellis squares are worked in dark green, Appletons crewel wool no 904; this is then secured with small stitches at each intersection. The basic trellis is overlaid with a second trellis in Appletons crewel wool no. 905. Where these threads all cross a small stitch is woven over the top trellis under the base trellis to give little circles in Appletons crewel wool no. 298.

18 The right-hand large leaf has a basic trellis, worked in Appletons crewel wool no. 904 and the securing stitches in no. 905, with a pattern of four French knots, used in a chequered effect, worked in no. 298.

19 The turnovers of the central leaves are worked in shaded burden stitch. The laid lines are put down in the darkest shade, Appletons crewel wool no. 295 and the burden stitches are worked from light to dark at the base of the turnover in nos. 291, 292, 293 and 295.

20 The central leaves and turnovers are then worked in whipped chain stitch. The chain is worked in Appletons crewel wool no. 295 and it is whipped with no. 904.

21 The large base leaf is worked last as it encases the whole of the motif and comes over all the other shapes. Work a split stitch on the top edge of this leaf against the previous work. This edge is then worked in a single row of long and short, using Appletons crewel wool no. 293.

22 The base of the leaf is then filled with tiny seeding stitches using Appletons crewel wool nos. 901 and 902. These should be almost as wide as they are long and no two should lie in the same direction.

23 The bottom edge of the leaf is then outlined in twisted chain stitch using Appletons crewel wool no. 905.

STITCH DIAGRAM

1 *Buttonhole stitch 292, 293, 295, 296, 298*

2 *Block shading 903, 904, 905*

3 *Stem stitch 292, 293, 295*

4 *Long and short stitch 292, 293, 295, 296, 298*

5 *Block shading 291, 292, 293, 903, 904, 905*

6 *Long and short stitch 292, 293, 904, 905*

7 *Chequered filling 292, 293, 902, 903*

8 *Coral stitch 904*

9 *Heavy chain stitch 295*

10 *Bullion knots 295*

11 *Satin stitch 295*

12 *Coral stitch 296*

13 *Detatched chain stitch 293, whipped with 902*

14 *Cretan stitch 904*

15 *Vandyke stitch 904*

16 *Chain stitch 292, 293, 295, 296*

17 *Squared filling base grid 904, upper grid 905, woven circle 298*

18 *Squared filling base grid 904, securing stitches 905, French knots 298*

19 *Burden stitch, laid lines 295, top stitches 291, 292, 293, 295*

20 *Whipped chain stitch chain 295, whip with 904*

21 *Long and short stitch 293*

22 *Seeding 901, 902*

23 *Twisted chain stitch 905*

FISH SAMPLER

For a completely different look to crewel work, we have chosen a fish design. The design potential of the underwater world is just incredible and you can develop simple design ideas by looking at the structure, texture and beautiful markings of fish. To give movement to the rather solid bodies of fish, add fins with a feathery edge and incorporate moving weed into the area around the fish to create a less static design. A hand-dyed background has been used here which helps to give depth to the whole design. In some areas coton perle and stranded cotton have been added to give a shiny look to the fish.

Materials

- The background fabric is a hand-dyed white cotton satin. This firm fabric does not require a backing cloth. Allow a little extra fabric for shrinkage when dyeing. The fabric is first washed and ironed then pleated tightly and placed lengthways in a square plastic bowl. Three jars of made-up fabric dye are prepared - lemon yellow, turquoise and blue. These dyes are then dribbled over the fabric, lemon yellow at the top, turquoise across the centre and blue at the base. When all the colours have run sufficiently to give the desired effect, rinse well and hang up to dry. When damp dry, press well
- The threads used are: Appletons crewel wool nos. 968, 158, 643, 831, 524, 522, 876, 991 and 331a for the fish; Appletons crewel wool nos. 254, 253, 251a and 331a for the weed; Anchor stranded cotton nos. 881, 337 and 338 for the fish; DMC no. 8 coton perle nos. 397, 186, 150, 1034 and 216 for the fish; and DMC no. 8 coton perle no. 265 for the weed
- Crewel needles nos. 5, 6 and 7 or chenille needle no. 18

Preparation

1 Mount the dyed background fabric on to a square peg frame (see page 10).

2 Draw the design on to good quality tracing paper and prick (see page 13).

3 Mark the centre of the design with a pencil line both ways, so it can then be lined up with a centre tack line on the background fabric.

4 Pounce and paint the design on to the background fabric (see pages 13–14).

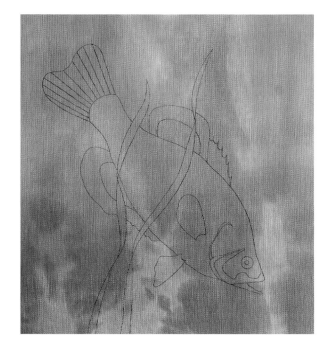

Fish Sampler worked by Jennifer Malone.

Instructions

Make sure the frame is braced very tightly with string. Once this is done, work can begin. Always work underneath shapes of the design first.

1 The tail is worked in rows of different line stitches, using DMC no. 8 coton perle, as listed (see stitch plan). From left to right:

a one row of running stitch in no. 150;

b double herringbone stitch in nos. 1034 and 216, chain stitch outline in no. 216;

c two rows of running stitch in no. 1034;

d knotted purl stitch in no. 1034 with outline in running stitch nos. 216, 1034 and 186 threaded with no. 150;

e two rows of running stitch in no. 216;

f herringbone stitch in nos. 1034 and 186 threaded with no. 216, outline in chain stitch no. 216;

g single running stitch in no. 216;

h running stitch in nos. 216, 1034 and 186, laced in no. 1034, outlined as d;

i two rows of running stitch in no. 216;

j one row of chain stitch in no. 216;

k one row of running in no. 150.

2 Work the fins. The centre section is worked in wave stitch in DMC no. 8 coton perle nos. 216, 1034 and 150, shading from light green to dark blue.

3 The centre section of the left fin is worked in a chequered filling shading as 2, using nos. 150, 1034 and 216.

4 Work the small right-hand fin in a chequered filling in cross stitch on top, using nos. 150, 1034 and 216.

5 Outline in stem stitch in no. 524.

6 Long and short shading is used on the outside of 2 and 3, working shades from light to dark, nos. 522, 524, 831 and 643, over a split stitch worked on the design line. This split stitch is worked on both edges of the shape to raise the work over the inside filling stitches.

STITCH DIAGRAM

1 *From left to right:*

a *1 row of running stitch in 150*

b *double herringbone stitch in 1034 and 216, chain stitch outline in 216*

c *2 rows of running stitch in 1034*

d *knotted purl 57 in 1034 with outline in running stitch 216, 1034 and 186, threaded with 150*

e *2 rows of running stitch in 216*

f *herringbone stitch in 1034, 186 threaded with 216, outline in chain stitch 216*

g *single running stitch in 216*

h *running stitch in 216, 1034, 186, laced in 1034, outlined as d*

i *2 rows of running stitch in 216*

j *1 row of chain stitch in 216*

k *1 row of running stitch in 150*

2 *Wave stitch in 216, 1034, 150*

3 *Chequered filling with cross stitch on top 150, 1034, 216*

4 *Chequered filling with cross stitch on top 150, 1034, 216*

5 *Stem stitch in 524*

6 *Long and short stitch 522, 524, 831, 643*

7 *Stem stitch in 254, 253, 251A, 265*

8 *Square filling grid 1034, second grid 643, third grid 216*

9–10 *Squared filling grid in 968, 158, 643, filling stitches in 216, 1034, 643, 397, 186, 524, 331A*

11–12 *Buttonhole stitch and Vandyke in 524, 876, 991, 397, 331A, 881, 337, 338*

13 *Laid work grid 150, filling 1034, 186, outline stem stitch 150, 186*

14 *Block shading in 643, 831, 524, 150, 522, 876, 186, outline in stem stitch 150, 186*

15 *Outline tail and body in stem stitch 186, 150, 1034, 216*

16–17 *Open chain stitch 397*

18 *Long and short stitch without split stitch 524, 522, 876*

19 *Raised stem band 1034, 186, 876, 524*

20 *Spider's web in 988, whipped with 876, 522, small highlight 397*

21 *Raised stem band in 254, 253, 251A, 331A, 265*

22 *Seeding in own colour choice*

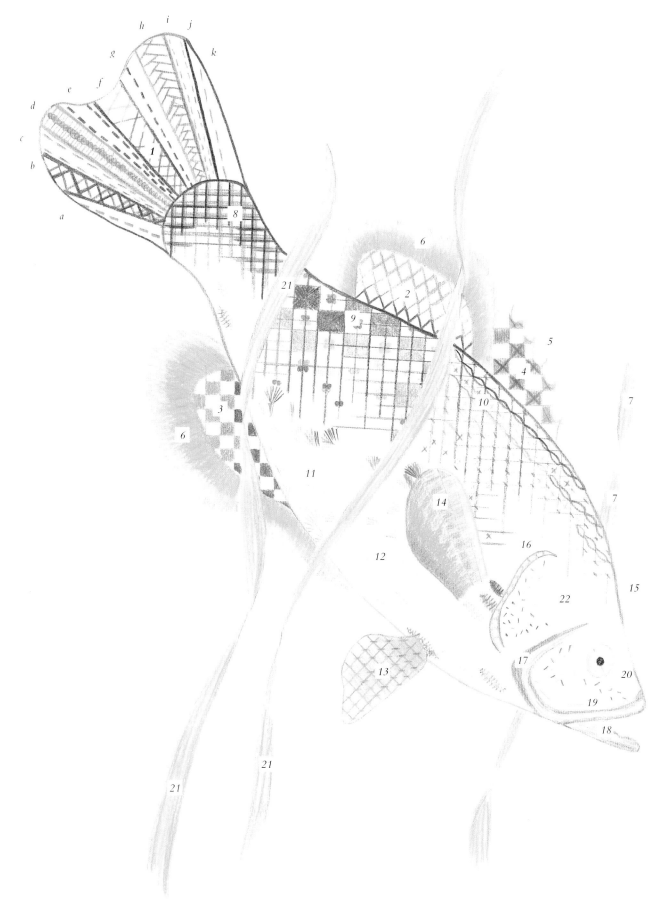

7   Work the weed behind the fish in rows of shaded green stem stitch, in nos. 254, 253, 251a and 265.

8, 9 and 10 The back of the fish is a combination of three different squared fillings using a random length to the stitches. The first grid uses no. 1034, the second grid no. 643 and the third grid no. 216. The squared filling grid uses nos. 968, 158 and 643. We have also introduced coton perle to give a splash of shiny colour in the French knots, satin stitches and whipping stitches, using nos. 216, 1034, 643, 397, 186, 524 and 331a.

11 and 12 The underbelly is worked in grouped buttonhole through the Vandyke stitch at the throat, changing the colours of stranded cotton as you work. It would be helpful to thread up a needle of each shade to be used, as the colours are mixed within the stitch in some places. The colours used are nos. 524, 876, 991, 397, 331a, 881, 337 and 338.

13 Laid work is used for this small fin with a crossbar on the top. Outline in stem stitch.

14   The centre small fin is worked in block shading using two colours in the three centre rows. The block shading is stitched in nos. 643, 831, 524, 150, 522, 876 and 186, and the outline in stem stitch using nos. 150 and 186.

15 Outline the tail and body in stem stitch using nos. 186, 150, 1034 and 216.

16 and 17 The gill covers are worked in open chain stitch in no. 397.

18 The lower lip is worked in long and short without split stitch, using nos. 524, 522 and 876.

19 The top lip is worked in raised stem band, changing the colours, using nos. 1034, 186, 876 and 524.

20 The eye is worked in a shaded spider's web in no. 988 whipped with nos. 876 and 522, with a small highlight of no. 397.

21 To get a raised effect on the two pieces of weed that the lie over the fish, we have used raised stem band, stitching in nos. 254, 253, 251a, 331a and 265. Take the base stitches slightly over the paint line to ensure it is covered by the top stem stitches.

22 Work seeding around the eye and gill in your own choice of colour.

IRIS

Crewel work is traditionally carried out in crewel wools, but crewel work techniques can just as well be carried out in stranded cottons and other threads, and this will give slightly more advanced skill for this project. To give another dimension to the work, the linen design areas have been painted with colour fun dyes.

Materials

- Background fabric to take dyes
- Colour fun dyes in the following colours: for the flower, a mixture of purple, blue and red; for the leaves, a mixture of green blue and yellow; and for the stamens/pollen, yellow and red
- A square peg frame or deep-sided ring frame
- Crewel needles nos. 8-10
- Tie-dyed threads in mauve and green; Anchor Marlitt no. 816; DMC flower thread nos. 2394, 2210, 2469 and 2394; Anchor stranded cotton nos. 109, 110, 111 and 266; and Anchor Nordin no. 109, Danish flower thread nos. 506, 505

Preparation

1 Dress the frame with the background fabric (see page 10)
2 Prick and pounce your design on to the background (see page 13)
3 Paint the outlines with a very fine line.
4 Using the dyes fairly thinly, mix the colours for the areas to be worked, painting fabric as design.

Instructions

1 The top left petal is stitched in burden stitch, worked slightly more openly than the Jacobean leaf sampler to show the dye. Work the base stitch in Anchor Nordin no. 109. The top stitches are shaded.

For the darkest, use DMC flower thread no. 2394; for the medium shade, use twisted hand-dyed rayon; and for the lightest, use Anchor Marlitt no. 816.

2 The top middle petal has a long and short edge in the following threads: single thread of DMC flower thread nos. 2394 and 2210; double thread of Anchor stranded cotton nos. 111, 110 and 109; and single thread of Anchor Marlitt no. 816. Split stitch the edge of the petal in a medium shade of Anchor stranded cotton. Thread up six needles with the shades for the long and short, and work the edge over the split stitch. Lengthen the Marlitt stitches with a second row. Seed the lower part of the petal with the same colour groupings as the long and short edge, working the darkest at the base; as you work up the sewing is less dense.

3 For the left leaf use dark green hand-dyed rayon threads, double thread of Anchor stranded cotton no. 266 and single thread of Danish flower thread no. 506. Work in stem stitch lines, working round the edge, with broken lines inside with a whipped back stitch to give shadow.

4 Use the same threads for the main stem as for the left leaf, adding DMC flower thread 2469 and dropping dark green hand-dyed rayon threads. Chain stitch round the edge, shaded chain in the middle with stem either side.

5-6 The right leaf is worked as the left, using dark and

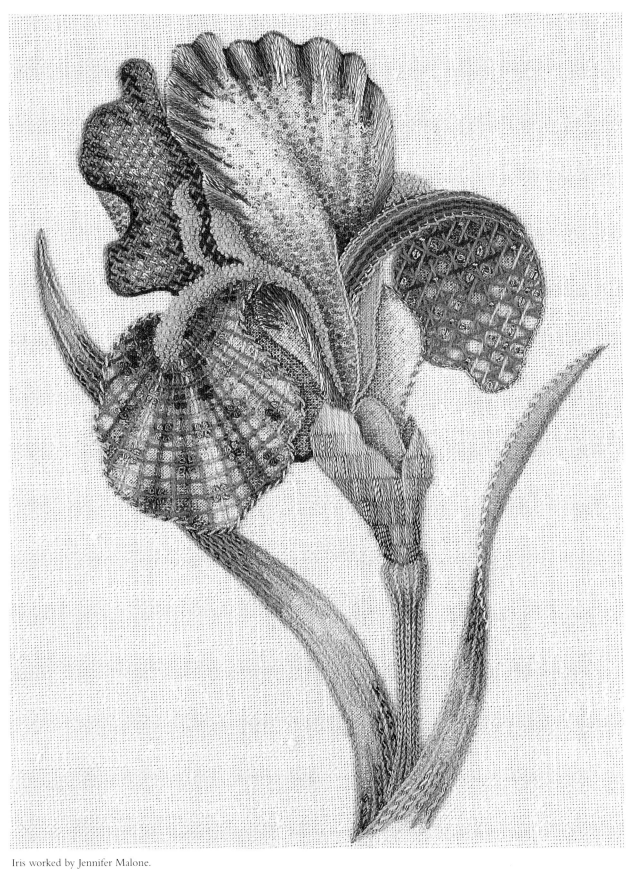

Iris worked by Jennifer Malone.

medium hand-dyed threads, Danish flower thread nos. 505 and 506, Anchor stranded 266 and DMC flower thread 2469.

7 The left front petal is a squared filling, the vertical lines angle into the centre and the horizontal lines are laid round the shape at 45 degrees to the vertical lines. Change shades to give a wavy effect on the petal; the colour change takes place under small tying-down stitches on the crossbars. The colours used are single thread DMC flower thread nos. 2394 and 2210; double thread of Anchor stranded cotton no. 111; single thread of Anchor Nordin no. 109. The pattern is worked in French knots using single and double thread in Anchor Marlitt no. 816, medium hand-dyed twisted rayon and DMC flower thread no. 2394.

8 The right-hand petal is a basic crossbar filling overlaid and interleaved with a second grid changing the shades to give shadow. The pattern is worked in small cross stitches and detached chain stitch. The grid colours are Anchor Nordin no. 109, two strands of Anchor stranded cotton no. 111 and DMC flower thread no. 2210. The pattern is worked in Anchor Marlitt no. 816.

9 The turnover is worked in raised stem band using the colours used in the petal.

10 The pollen areas of the petals are worked in shaded French knots using Anchor stranded cottons nos. 297 and 306. The knots are worked so a small amount of fabric dye shows between them.

11 The small petals in the centre have a long and short edge highlighted with Anchor Marlitt no. 816.

12 The calyxes are worked in black shading using a dark coloured hand-dyed thread, Danish flower thread nos. 505 and 506, Anchor stranded cotton no. 266 and DMC flower thread no. 2469. The colours are mixed as the stem progresses.

13 Neaten the edges of the design with the appropriate shades, using stem stitch, whipped back stitch or threaded backstitch.

STITCH DIAGRAM

1 *Burden stitch, DMC flower thread 2394, hand dyed twisted rayon thread, dark Anchor Marlitt 816, Anchor Nordin 109, all single*

2 *Long and short and seeding, DMC flower thread 2394, 2210, Anchor stranded 111, 110, 109, Anchor Marlitt 816, Flower and Marlitt single stranded double*

3 *Stem stitch and threaded back stitch, hand-dyed twisted rayon thread dark, Anchor stranded 266, Danish flower thread 506, Flower and rayon single stranded double*

4 *Chain and stem stitch DMC flower thread 2469, Anchor stranded 266, Danish flower thread 506, Flower thread single, stranded used double*

5–6 *Stem stitch and threaded back stitch, hand-dyed twisted rayon thread dark and medium, Anchor stranded 266, Danish flower thread 506, 505, DMC flower thread 2469*

7 *Squared filling: DMC flower thread 2394, 2210, Anchor stranded 111, Anchor Nordin 109*
The pattern: Anchor Marlitt 816, Hand-dyed twisted rayon, medium, DMC flower 2394

8 *Squared filling: Anchor Nordin 109, Anchor stranded 111, DMC flower thread 2210, The pattern: Anchor Marlitt 816*

9 *Raised stem band, base lines: Anchor Nordin 109 Stem stitch lines: DMC flower thread 2210, 2394, Anchor Marlitt 816, Anchor Nordin 109, Anchor stranded 111*
Flower: Nordin, use single stranded, use double

10 *French knots, Anchor stranded 297, 306, used single*

11 *Long and short Anchor stranded 111, 110, Anchor Marlitt 816, all used single*

12 *Block shading: Danish flower thread 505, 506, DMC flower thread 2469, Hand-dyed twisted rayon, dark, medium, Anchor stranded 266*
Flower: rayon single stranded double

13 *Outlines: use appropriate line stitches (i.e. stem stitch, whipped back stitch, threaded back stitch)*

ABSTRACT WINDOWS

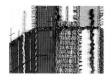

This last crewel work piece gives a modern look to a very traditional technique. The inspiration for this piece has come from a study of windows. Architecture is an amazing design source and all embroiderers would do well to collect material relating to the various aspects of buildings old and new. The square and linear patterns produced from our window studies lent themselves to the lovely Jacobean square fillings and line stitches.

Materials

- A square peg frame
- Preshrunk calico for the backing
- Silk dupion for the background
- Pieces of fabric for appliqué to fray out
- Bondaweb
- Anchor Marlitt nos. 822, 1032, 859, 1055 and 854; chenille threads variegated to co-ordinate with applied fabrics
- A range of crewel needles or chenille needles

Preparation

1   Mount the silk dupion background on to the square frame already dressed with preshrunk calico (see page 10).
2   Transfer your design on to the background using the prick and pounce method (see page 14).
3   Cut out pieces of applied fabric allowing enough fabric to fray out on appropriate edges (areas 1-5 on chart).
4   Iron Bondaweb on to the unfrayed areas of the fabrics to prevent unwanted fraying.

Instructions

Refer to the stitch plan which identifies the thread numbers.

1   Slightly slacken the frame and apply the fabrics with small catching-down stitches. Then retighten the frame.
2   Fray out the silk threads from the applied fabrics and lay these on two of the squares. Secure these threads with a laid trellis in one strand of Marlitt.
3   Work the remaining trellis patterns and fillings in one strand of Marlitt over some of the window material shapes.
4   Fill the shape with random satin stitch blocks with one strand of Marlitt.
5   Decorate with open raised stem band with one strand of Marlitt.
6   Work straight stitch lines to indicate the window panes and to connect some blocks of colour with one strand of Marlitt.
7   The outlines are worked in varying thicknesses of threads. One thread of chenille and Marlitt in one, two or three threads. The stitches used for these lines of stitching are puffy couching, twisted chain, whipped chain stitch, stem stitch, heavy chain stitch and herringbone over chenille.

(Continued on page 76.)

Abstract Windows worked by Melissa Cheeseman.

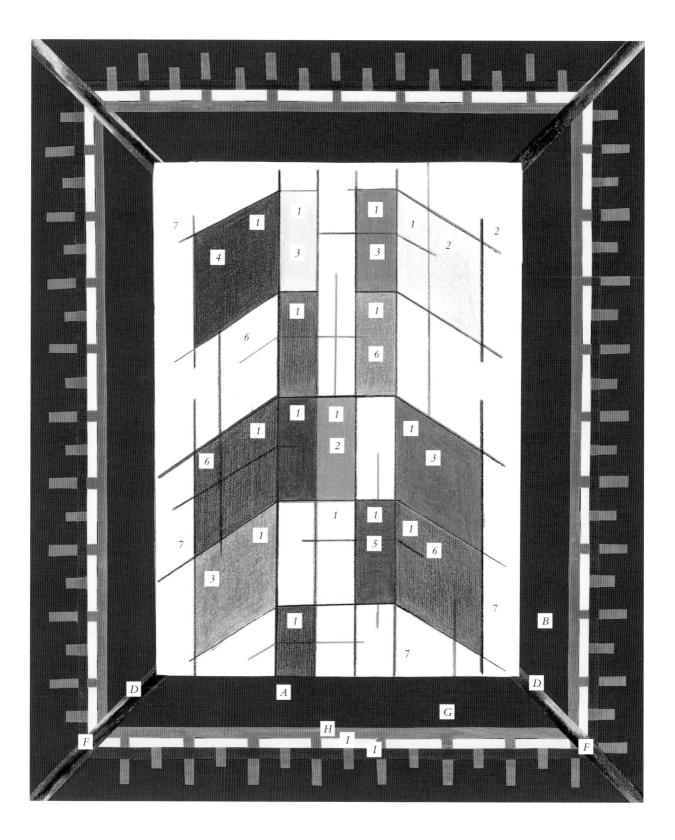

STITCH DIAGRAM

1 *Apply silk fabrics*

2 *Silk threads held with square filling, Marlitt 822, 1032, 854*

3 *Trellis fillings, Marlitt 859, 1032, Square filling, Marlitt 859, 822, 1032, 854*

4 *Random satin stitch blocks 859, 1032, 1055*

5 *Open stem band, Marlitt 1055*

6 *Straight lines worked in Marlitt 822, 1032, 859, 1055, 854*

7 *Outlines: couching, twisted chain, whipped chain, stem stitch, heavy chain, herringbone over chenille, Marlitt 822, 859, 1032, 1055, 854*

A *Navy fabric tacked along here*

B *Strips of navy fabric*

C *Pin back border to here*

D *Mitre corners*

E *Long and short stitch outer edge of navy fabric*

F *Herringbone in Marlitt over chenille wool*

G *Tack guideline 2 cm (¼ in) from the embroidered section*

H *Work knotted pearl stitch using strips of orange fabric*

I *Weave through arms of stitch using a gold and red silk fabric*

Border

A Tack round the centre section to mark the outside edge.

B Cut strips of navy blue fabric with a 5 cm (2 inch) seam allowance. Fold under a turning of 12 mm (½ inch). Tack along the crease line. Place the two tack lines together with the right sides together. The border fabric will be covering the centre section. Tack in it place. Backstitch along the tack line. Fold back the fabric to create a neat edge to the centre embroidery. Repeat this process on the other three sides.

C Pin back the border so that it is tight.

D Now mitre the corners.

E Long and short stitch the outside edge of the border material (as when mounting fabric).

F Slip stitch the mitred corners and decorate with herringboned chenille wool.

G Tack a line 2 cm (¾ inch) from the centre section.

H This line is used as a guide for the edge of the knotted pearl stitch which is worked on the border. The stitch is worked with strips of orange fabric 12 mm (½ inch) wide. Instead of the knot sitting in the middle of the stitch, push it towards the centre; alternate the length of the outside edge of the stitch.

I Through the long ends of the knotted pearl stitch, weave strips of gold and red coloured fabrics.

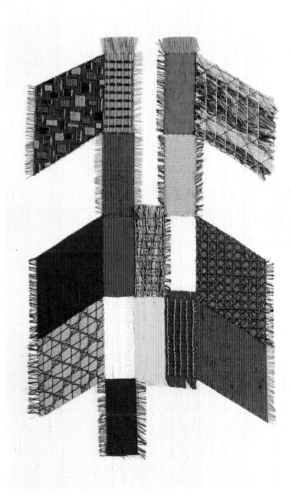

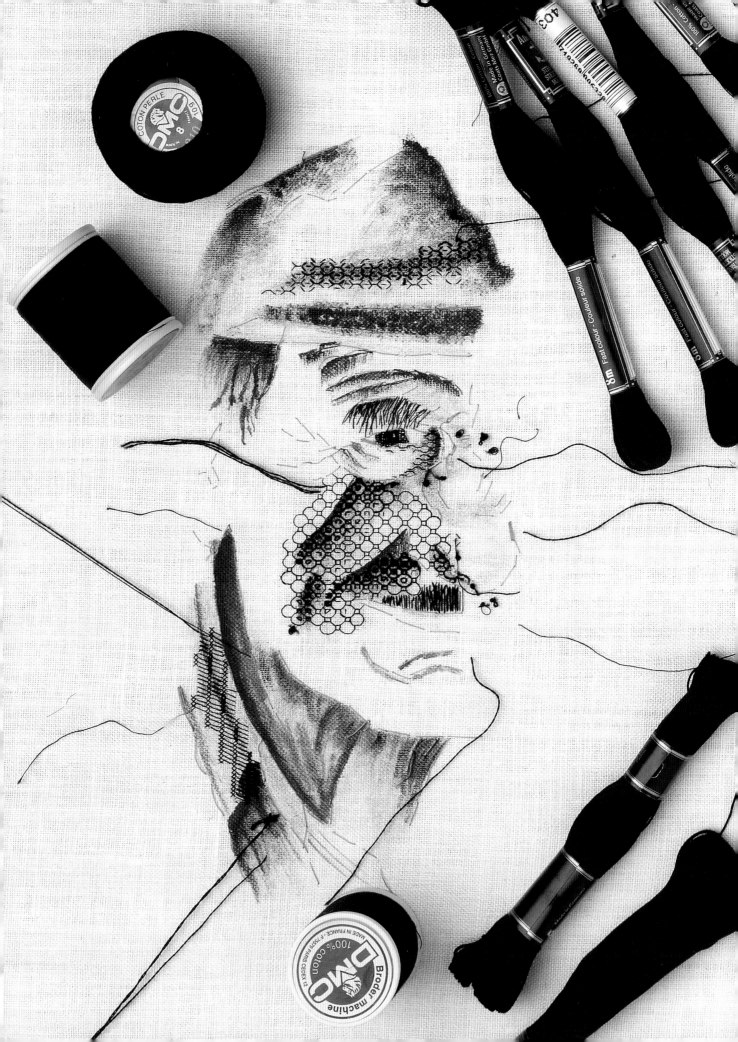

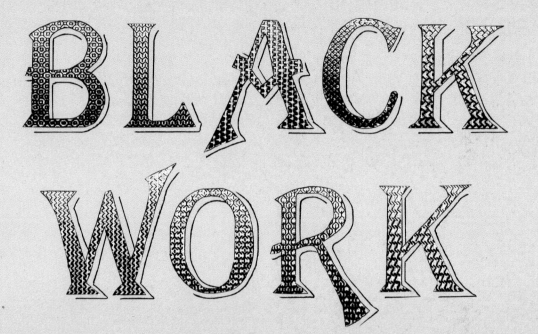

INTRODUCING BLACKWORK

It is not possible to date the first piece of blackwork, but it seems likely that the technique had its roots in Spain in the fifteenth century. It was at this time that the Spanish, who had been under the domination of the Moors, started to produce the beautiful repeat pattern borders in double running stitch. These found their way to England and were worked on to the edges of cuffs and ruffs. The noblemen and women of the time had their portraits painted showing this work and the borders became known as the Holbein stitch, because many of the pictures were the work of Hans Holbein.

Katharine of Aragon, the first wife of Henry VIII, learned Spanish blackwork from her mother, Queen Isabella of Spain and this meant she would encourage the use of blackwork in the English Court when she married Henry. Anne of Cleves brought Flemish designs to England when she became Henry's fourth wife and in fact different types of black on white embroidery were emerging from various European countries at this time. Needlewomen were encouraged by the printing of pattern books; these books took their design sources from herbals, nature books and engravings.

The designers of blackwork on costume were still influenced by the quatrefoils of the fifteenth-century *Opus Anglicanum* church embroideries and instead of the inset religious figures, the design was scaled right down and the trailing stem designs were taken round flowers, fruits, birds and insects. These were then embroidered with counted black diaper patterns and highlighted with gold thread. The trailing stems were often worked in plaited braid stitch. These all-over designs were embroidered for use on bodices and sleeves, and would have been made to be removed and put into other garments when the original garment wore out.

Embroidery was a very expensive prized possession and would have been well cared for. Some portraits show the use of a protective transparent linen gauze material placed over the embroidery. Blackwork was not restricted to costume; it was also found on household linens and cushions.

Apart from Holbein stitch or double running and the use of diaper patterns in foliated and natural designs, the third type of blackwork treatment was 'black seeding' known as 'speckling'. These were a later treatment of blackwork embroidery, appearing at the end of the sixteenth century. Here the embroidered design was shaded with small seeding stitches, stitched to give form and shading to the pattern being embroidered. The tiny black stitches are used as an artist might use a pencil to shade, seem close together to give shadow and more spread out to give highlights. This technique was particularly suitable when used on the various animals and creatures incorporated in the later designs.

Great quantities of blackwork would have been carried out for well over a hundred years, and many items were recorded in the inventories of the large houses, who employed their own embroiderers. It was also well recorded by the portrait painters of the time, whose patrons would be expected to have their portraits painted in their very expensive embroidered clothes. These pieces of embroidery would have cost a great deal of money and only the very wealthy would be able to afford blackwork embroidery on their clothes.

Museums and great houses have many examples of samplers, costumes and furnishings in blackwork for us to study and, of course, the Victoria and Albert Museum has a whole range of items of this period. Sadly the black silk thread used had a tendency to rot; this is mostly brought

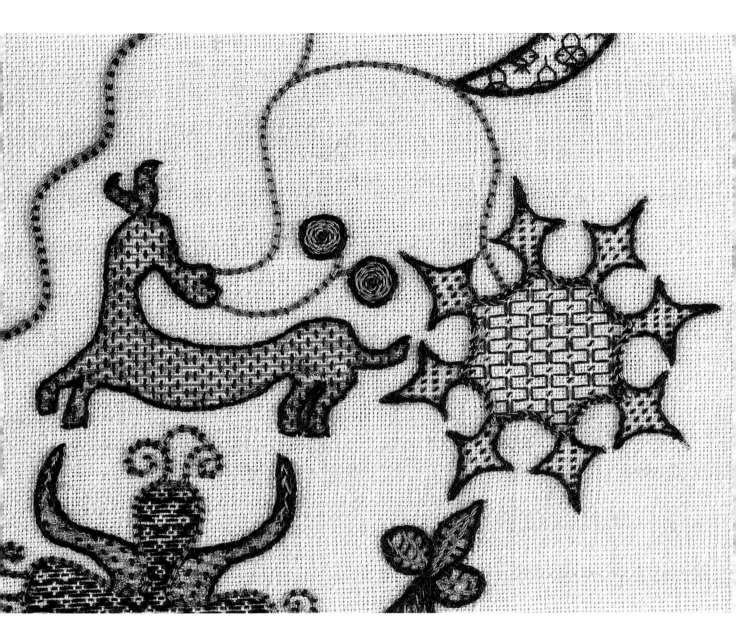

A piece of blackwork-style embroidery, worked about 1940, RSN Collection.

about by the iron filings used in the mordant when dyeing the silk black. It was not unusual however to find this technique carried out in a red thread.

The silver gilt thread, used in different ways to enhance the work, was a silver wire coated with gold. This could be flattened and wrapped round a silk core, or spun on a special machine to make a purl thread and stitched like a bead. Gold thread was also used in the needle. Gold spangles were often used on the background of blackwork embroidery to add a sparkle.

The background material used was linen. A very fine linen cambric was used for ruffs, collars and cuffs and a Holland linen was used for shirts and skirts, jackets, caps and household items.

Needles would have been made of wire in the reign of Henry VIII, but by the time Elizabeth had come to the throne steel needles had become available, and this must have made the execution of this fine technique easier to carry out.

APPROACH TO BLACKWORK

When the size and type of project has been chosen a suitable fabric can be selected. Blackwork is very dependent on an evenly woven background fabric for the success of the patterns used. The variety of evenweave fabrics available today is excellent. They can be linen, cotton, wool or silk. The finer the fabric, the more delicate the patterns appear. Large bold designs work well on coarse fabric but small or intricate designs need a fine count of fabric.

The thread chosen can be one of a variety of different types of fibres and also could be a colour other than black, although black is still the choice of most embroiderers. Whatever colour is chosen it is useful to collect a large range of thicknesses of thread.

The overall shaded effect of blackwork embroidery today can be achieved in two ways: first by working the chosen patterns in different weights of thread and secondly by omitting or adding stitches to the lines of the pattern. By combining these two techniques more possibilities are presented to the embroiderer. Touches of gold thread can be added to the patterns, couched or sewn into areas of the design. When all the patterns are worked, outline stitches can be added if and where needed. These can be stitches like stem stitch, chain stitch and back stitch.

Design sources for blackwork, like all other embroidery, will to some extent have to take into account the nature of the technique but, as you will see from the topics chosen for this book, most things are possible. It is helpful to have pattern areas that are not too cut up, so the repeat on the diaper patterns is not too difficult to count out.

As with all other embroidery projects, it is wise to keep a small sketchbook in which to collect ideas and sketches. Always have this with you to jot down ideas and make little drawings. We all think we can remember things we see and like, but we rarely do. You don't have to be a wonderful artist to jot down ideas of colour, shape and even texture. Collect cuttings from papers and magazines and you will be amazed at how often you will draw on these for ideas. Take photographs in black and white of objects and patterns that interest you. The

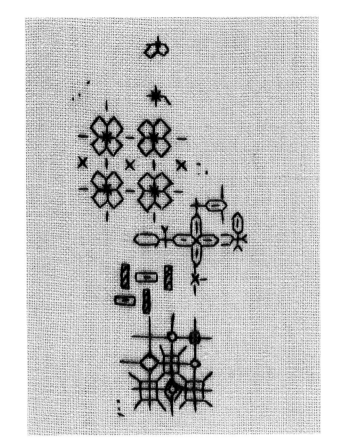

medium of black and white photography will give you immediate tonal shading which will suggest the weight of stitches and patterns for the various areas of your chosen subject.

Black and white can be very stark used in solid quantities, but by adding and leaving out stitches in the diaper patterns, the areas of design can produce many weights of tone between black and white.

Designs can be cut or torn from newsprint, the black and white of the print gives an immediate empathy to blackwork embroidery. Cut pleasing shapes from a paper, then arrange and stick them down on a sheet of white paper. Add detail and linear areas to the design with felt-tip pens of different widths. These lines can be self coloured line stitches or gold thread if appropriate to the design.

Blackwork is always worked on a frame. Small projects could possibly be worked in a deep-sided ring

A blackwork sampler in red, seventeenth century, RSN Collection.

An early twentieth-century reproduction of an Elizabethan blackwork design.

frame, but mostly a square peg frame will give the correct tension for good even stitchery (see page 10). The evenweave fabric is not mounted on a backing fabric. To transfer the design on to your fabric, see Method B, page 14. The needles used for blackwork are blunt tapestry needles for working the diaper pattern and crewel needles for working the outline stitches.

There are hundreds of variations of blackwork patterns, all made up of two different elements: small enclosed geometric shapes and small pointed patterns made with straight stitches. These two elements can be used individually to create repeated geometric shapes, or repeated pointed patterns. They can also be used together to achieve both a geometric and pointed pattern.

With the information on pages 151-3 you will be able to make hundreds of lovely diaper patterns, although probably six to ten will be enough to work most pieces of blackwork. Try developing some patterns of your own from the basic shapes shown. It is a good idea to try out patterns in a small ring frame on the fabric you are going to work your project. You will soon be completely absorbed with the variety of patterns you can work. Choose patterns that will suit your design - round diaper patterns to go in round pattern shapes, pointed patterns to go in serrated areas. It is also helpful to choose patterns that will allow stitches to be added or left out. After a short while of trying out patterns you will probably have invented one of your own. Work with small stitches over two threads of your linen. (Patterns can be worked over more threads, as long as the total number is even.)

Blackwork stitches look good combined with other techniques, the only criterion is that the background needs to have an even weave. This technique could be used for appliqué if this is appropriate to your design. Small sections could be worked in a ring frame and then cut out and applied to an embroidery project.

So with the work framed up, the design tacked on and patterns tried out, you are now ready to begin your project. Blackwork is a technique suitable for all abilities and can give pleasure to all who try it out.

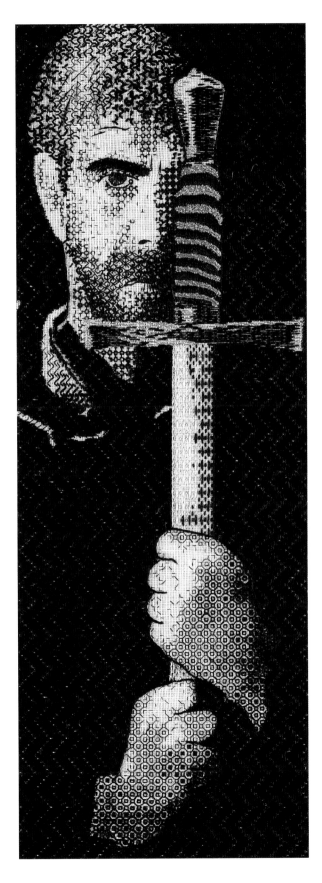

Hamlet, worked by a First Year Apprentice, Alexandra Lester, 1996, showing stitches covering the entire design area.

EXERCISE FOR BEGINNERS

A simple tile pattern is used again for this blackwork exercise. This gives small uncomplicated pattern areas which are ideal if you are trying blackwork for the first time. The sample was worked in one and two strands of black stranded cotton. All the patterns used are worked over two threads of linen. These could be drawn out on squared paper first if this makes them easier to follow. You could try developing your own patterns from some of the shapes included on pages 152-4.

Materials

- Any evenweave fabric can be used. We have used a linen 36 threads to 2.5 cm (1 inch). The finer the fabric the better the patterns look, but try not to choose a linen you will find too difficult to count. Mark the centre of your fabric with a tack line both ways
- Anchor black stranded cotton no. 403
- Tapestry needles no. 24 or 26, if available, and crewel needle no. 9
- A 25 cm (10-inch) ring frame with 2.5 cm (1-inch) sides to use with a floor stand, seat frame or table clamp

Preparation

1. Trace the design and ink it carefully on to tissue paper, marking the centre lines both ways. Lay the linen over the design, matching the centre lines.
2. Tack round the design lines very carefully in grey cotton. The tacking can be removed when the patterns are completed.
3. Mount the fabric into the ring frame.
4. Choose up to seven patterns and try them out on a spare piece of fabric.

Instructions

When you have chosen your patterns, work them in the shapes starting in the centre and working out.

1. The corner shapes could have four different patterns or two heavy patterns and two lighter ones in opposite corners.
2. The centre shape could have a lighter pattern than the corner shapes.
3. The petal shapes have been shaded in a simple way, working with one thread at the tips, to four threads at the base. Then add extra crosses to the squares at the base of the shapes to increase the density of the pattern.
4. Outline with two strands of stranded cotton in stem stitch.

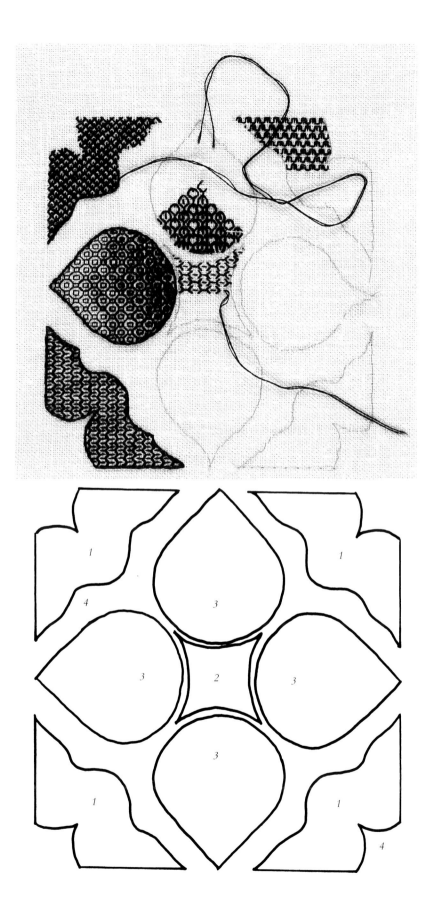

STITCH DIAGRAM

This exercise is worked in black stranded cotton

1   Corner shapes with the same pattern or four different patterns
2   Centre light pattern
3   Work in two different patterns shading using two threads at the bottom, one at the top
4   Outline in stem stitch in two strands

FUNGUS

Blackwork has the appearance of sketching with pen and ink on paper, so any subject that has an interesting shape when drawn and shaded will lend itself to the technique. This fungus is worked in just four blackwork patterns, but by varying the weight of thread and by adding and leaving out stitches when working the patterns, the shape and character of the fungus can be conveyed.

Materials

- A deep-sided ring frame or square peg frame
- Evenweave fabric 32 threads to 2.5 cm (1 inch)
- Tapestry needles nos. 24-26 and crewel needle no. 9
- Black stranded cotton no. 16 coton à broder, DMC black machine cotton no. 50

Preparation

1 Make a drawing of a fungus or similar small project.
2 Copy this design and shade up the subject with a soft pencil to show the shadows and highlights of the object.
3 Practise patterns on a spare piece of fabric.

Instructions

1 Trace the design on to tissue paper. Pin the tissue paper to the evenweave fabric. With a pale tacking cotton, stitch the design outline on to the background fabric. When all the lines have been tacked, tear away the tissue paper leaving the tacked design line.
2 Mount the fabric on your choice of frame.
3 Work your chosen patterns into your design.
4 When all the patterns are complete, remove the unwanted tacked design lines.
5 Outline where line stitches are needed, such as stem stitch, whipped chain stitch and whipped back stitch.

Fungus worked by Jennifer Malone.

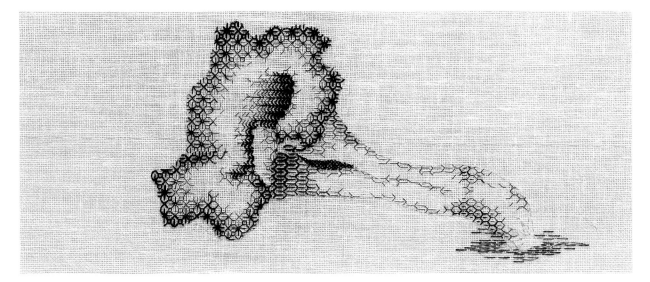

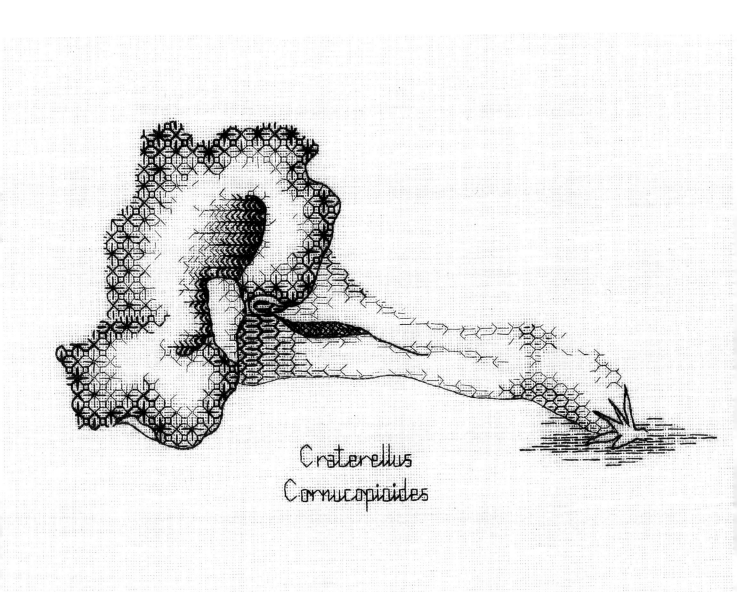

Craterellus
Cornucopioides

STITCH DIAGRAM

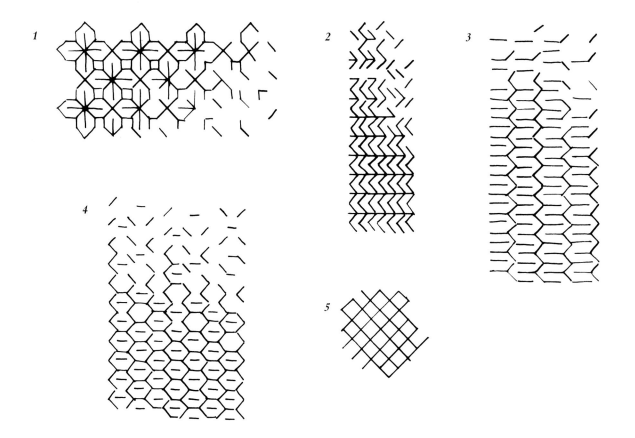

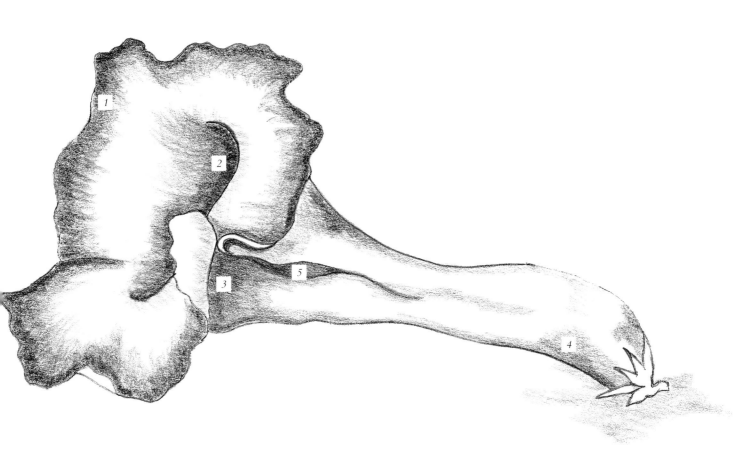

IRIS

Following on from the fungus used for the last project, we have used an iris, a slightly more complex shape. This has also given the opportunity to introduce a little gold thread. This piece of work is worked in 13 different patterns: round shapes for the petals, diagonal ones to complement the leaves. Take a good look at the way the pattern is broken down to give a frilling look to the large petals. Also note the outlining used only where hard emphasis is needed. Most flowers make good subjects for blackwork designs and you will probably prefer to draw your own. Make sure all your shapes are a reasonable size, to enable a repeat of the patterns you choose. Again we suggest you make a shaded drawing of your subject before you begin working.

Materials

- Evenweave fabric, 32 threads to 2.5 cm (1 inch). This will not be backed
- Deep-sided ring frame or small square peg frame
- Tapestry needles nos. 24-26, crewel needle no. 9 for outlines
- Black stranded cotton, one strand no. 16 coton à broder, machine gold thread and DMC black machine cotton no. 50

Preparation

1 Trace your design on to your linen using the tissue paper method (see page 14).
2 Mount the fabric on to your chosen frame.
3 On a spare piece of background fabric, try out a range of patterns to see the effect they give when worked.

Instructions

1 Work all the chosen patterns first, paying attention to shaded and highlighted areas by adding to and reducing the number of stitches used.
2 Outline where line stitches are needed, such as stem stitch and whipped back stitch.

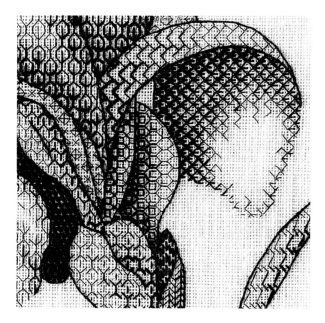

Iris worked by Jennifer Malone.

STITCH DIAGRAM

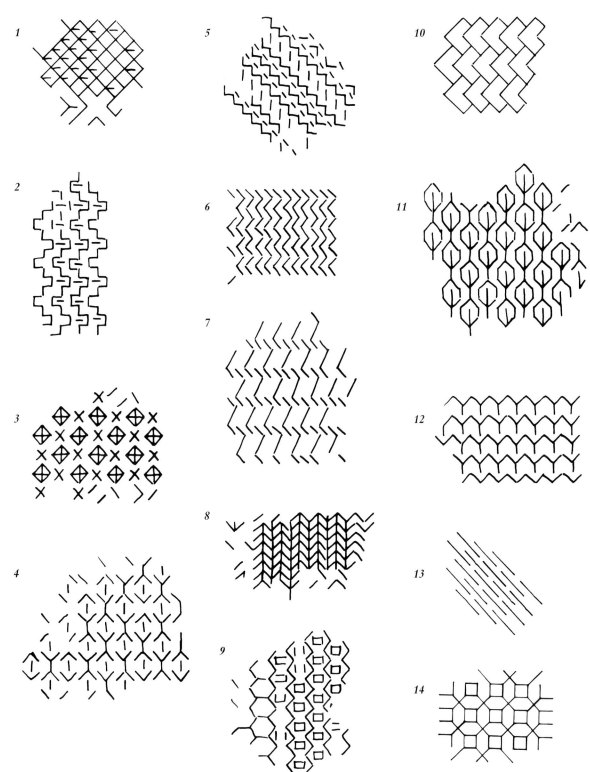

AGED FACE

Blackwork faces and figures that are worked at the Royal School have a great fascination for all who see the finished pieces at our open days and exhibitions. With a little experience and a good selection of patterns worked as a sample, any subject can be tackled provided the design detail is not too small. A shaded copy of the design is also a very helpful aid. The aged face we have worked in this section was worked in just seven blackwork patterns.

To add some subtle shading and another dimension to our face, a little black fabric paint is added to some areas of the design.

Materials
- Black fabric paint and stencil brush
- Evenweave linen 32 threads to 2.5 cm (1 inch). This will not need backing
- A square peg frame
- Tapestry needles nos. 24-26, crewel needle no. 9 for outlines
- Black stranded cotton, no. 16 coton à broder, DMC black machine cotton no. 50

Preparation
1 Transfer design on to fabric with tissue paper method (see page 14).
2 Add dye to selected areas using black fabric paint and stencil brush, use brush dry so the paint will not run. Build up paint areas with great care. Paint must not be overloaded as this will make the black areas too dark to count the threads. Allow to dry thoroughly.
3 Mount fabric on to square frame.
4 Practise a selection of patterns on spare fabric that is similar to the background.
5 Work patterns in design areas.

Aged Face worked by Margaret Dier.

Instructions

1 Number 1 stitch is used for the lines on the face and also for the stubble, but in a very fragmented way. Number 2 stitch is used for the areas around the eyes and nose, and two extra stitches are added to the centre of the pattern horizontally to darken the stitch. Number 3 stitch is used for the neck with two strands used to define the shadow and creased areas. Number 4 stitch is used for the shirt, changing the direction of the stitches on the various elements of the shirt. Number 5 stitch is used for the jumper, using an extra thread to pick out the folds. Number 6 stitch is used for the cap, using various weights of black thread or two strands of stranded cotton to give shadow. Number 7 stitch is used for the eye and ear.

2 When all the patterns are complete, work the outline where needed.

3 The hair and moustache are worked with random

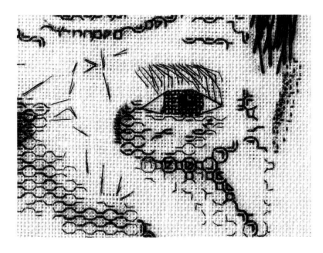

straight stitches, with stitches crossing in places. The hair is worked in two strands of stranded cotton. The eyebrows and moustache are worked in machine cotton. The top lip is worked in two strands of stranded cotton.

STITCH DIAGRAM

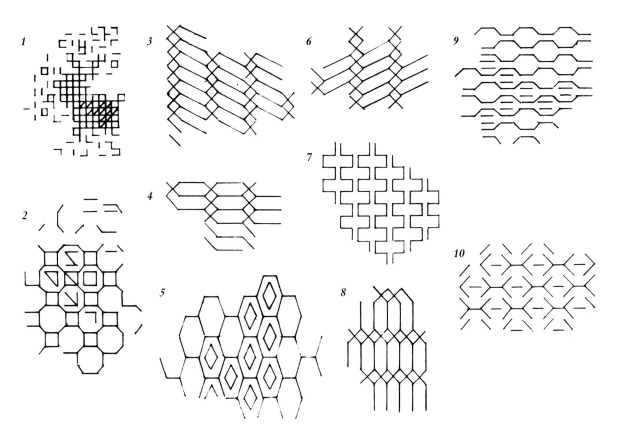

CRUMPLED PAPER

If you find it difficult to produce ideas for design, this must be one of the simplest ways so try it out. Crumple a large sheet of photocopying paper, then pop it into the photocopying machine. This will immediately produce an interesting pattern. Make several copies until you achieve the most interesting shapes. Trace this pattern and try some colourwashes with paints or crayons. Colourwash the background with acrylics or dyes.

Materials

- A square peg frame
- Background evenweave fabric 36 threads to 2.5 cm (1 inch)
- Acrylics or dyes
- Tapestry needle no. 26 and crewel needle no. 10
- Stranded cottons: in blue, DMC nos. 3810, 598 and 3808; in green, Anchor nos. 253 and 254, DMC no. 581; and in coral, Anchor nos. 341, 339 and 338. Use one and two strands

Preparation

1 Trace your design on to your linen using the tissue paper method (see page 14).
2 Colour the fabric with acrylics or dyes.
3 Mount the fabric on to a square peg frame.

Instructions

1 Using patterns already tried on previous projects, work from dark to light. Make use of the shades of the threads as well as increasing and decreasing the stitches in each pattern. Also vary the number of threads used: two strands for dark areas and one for light areas.

2 When the work is completed on the pattern areas, outline in stem stitch, chain stitch and whipped backstitch. Take care to match the outline colour to bring out the shapes that look best on top.

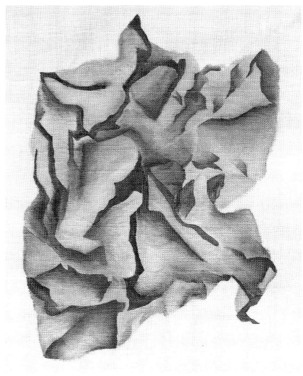

Crumpled Paper worked by Amanda Ewing

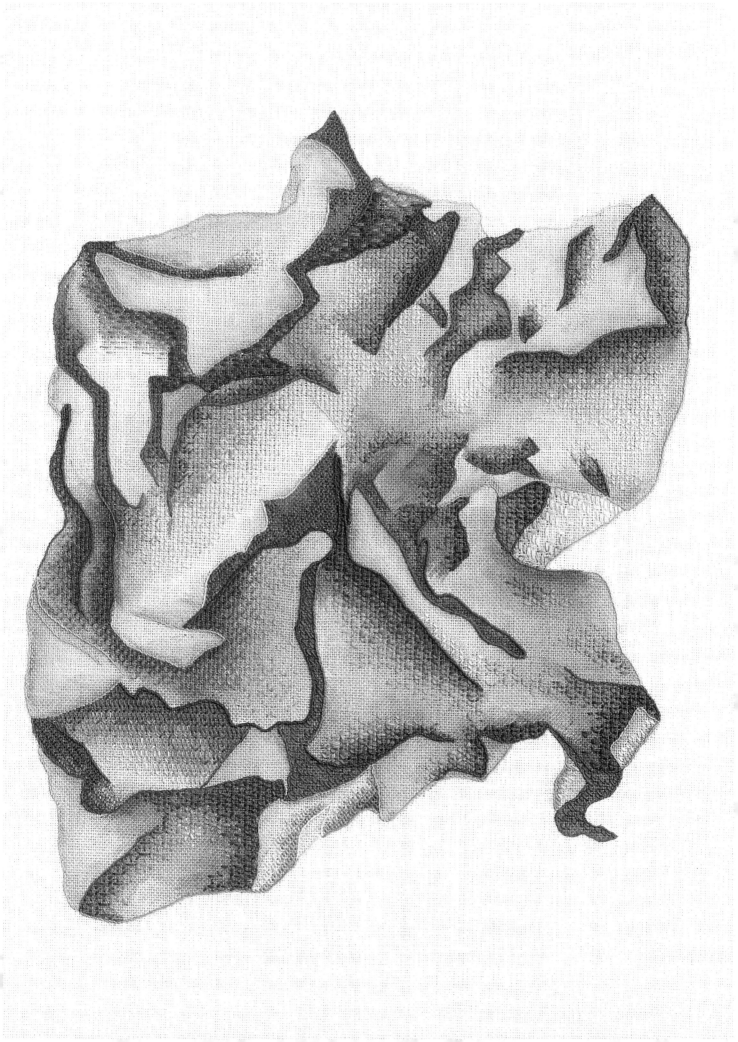

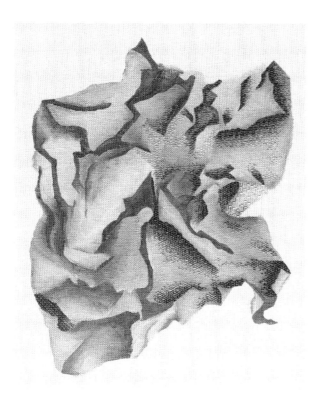

STITCH DIAGRAM

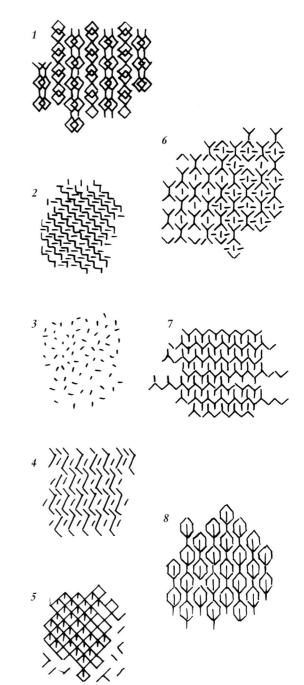

INTRODUCING GOLDWORK

Gold symbolizes perfection in everything, the very height of achievement. It is used to aid worship, to convey status and to portray wealth, and so it is with goldwork embroidery. All through recorded history, fabrics have been enhanced with precious jewels and gold threads, and many references to their uses on the garments and trappings of kings and emperors can be found in the annals of history. Several references to the use of gold threads can be found in the Bible.

Gold thread originally came from Asia, travelling with the silk merchants to Beirut, but after the secrets of silk production became known outside China, gold thread became more widely available in the West. It's use in the Mediterranean in the years after the birth of Christ became widespread and it could be found on vestments and clothes in countries like Egypt, Italy, Turkey, Greece and Cyprus.

The early thread was a silver wire covered with a gold coating, which could be drawn out to any thickness and still retain its gold coating. The thread could then be hammered flat and wound round a silk core for couching, or it could be spun and drawn through a series of holes in diminishing sizes until the thread was fine enough to spiral into bullions and purls, to be used as gold beads. The attraction of these threads was not just the gold colour, but the different textures the various threads produced, particularly when stitched over padding or couched to produce interesting plays of light on the thread.

The earliest surviving piece of English gold thread embroidery is the tenth-century stole and maniple of St Cuthbert, originally buried with him, but now preserved in Durham Cathedral. This exquisite piece of work has a ground of very fine couched gold threads to surround the finished embroidery.

Heraldic devices of the Middle Ages would have necessitated the employment of many embroiderers working with gold and silk on the coats of arms (or jupons) of the knights. The Black Prince's jupon, embroidered in the fourteenth century was hanging above his tomb in Canterbury Cathedral nearly 600 years after it was made. In 1954 the Royal School of Needlework made a replica of this wonderful historic garment in exactly the same way as the original was made. This now hangs above the tomb.

The Middle Ages brought the greatest period of Church embroidery and much of it goldwork, in what was known as 'English work' or *Opus Anglicanum*. The quality of this work was so high that orders came from all over Europe including the Vatican. The whole of the backgrounds of these vestments could be worked in underside couching in silver gilt threads. Many examples of this period can be found in the Victoria and Albert Museum. Probably the best known is the Syon Cope.

A wonderful fourteenth-century example of metal threadwork can be found in the Musée de Cluny in Paris. This early piece of English goldwork is part of a horse trapper belonging to Edward III. The workmanship of the two remaining passant leopards is quite outstanding. The couching flows in beautiful patterns over the animals, using a variety of threads in silver gilt couching and twists.

A new technique called *Or Nué* came into production in Europe in the fifteenth century and was mainly used on vestments. The gold thread was couched in pairs across a design drawn on to the background

Or Nué figure with tapestry shaded face, early twentieth century, RSN Collection.

Seal purse of Elizabeth 1, 1560. (Copyright British Museum).

fabric, and the design lines were picked out in gold or coloured silks while couching. The shading of drapery and architecture was achieved by the closeness of the couched stitches. This is a very beautiful but rather time-consuming technique.

After the *Opus Anglicanum* period came to an end, gold threads were used on the domestic embroideries of the Elizabethan era, particularly on items of blackwork and silk embroidery. Perhaps one of the most wonderful examples of sixteenth-century gold thread work has only recently been found in an attic. It is a velvet and gold embroidered purse which was made for the great seal of Elizabeth I in 1560, and it will be displayed in the British Museum. The techniques used on this purse are similar to those on ceremonial goldwork today. A beautiful padded English lion and Welsh dragon support the Royal Arms on a sea of spangles, encompassed by a beautiful border. This wonderful purse will be a must for

Part of a goldwork sampler, worked by Melissa Cheeseman during her apprenticeship. Melissa was the winner of the 1996 Gold and Silver Wyre Drawers Prize.

all goldworkers to study in years to come. Sadly, over the years, a great deal of goldwork was cut up, and reused or the gold thread was removed and melted down for money, so it is amazing when something as old and beautiful as this seal purse is discovered in such good condition and we are able to study the methods used 400 years ago.

Gold and metal threads were used quite extensively over eighteenth-century costume. The very flamboyant costumes in the English and Continental courts were often covered in silk shading and metal thread embroidery; the silk shaded flower designs were arranged on scroll borders of metal threads and the edges of the garments were often finished off with metallic laces. Waistcoats were sometimes entirely embroidered with metal threads using gold plate and purls, as well as couched threads and, of course, decorated with tiny gold spangles.

The Arts and Crafts Movement carried embroidery into the nineteenth century with wonderful designs produced by William Morris, Edward Burne-Jones, Walter Crane, Lewis Day and others, but not many used

gold threads to any great extent. However, in 1872 the Royal School of Needlework was founded and the school was lucky to receive encouragement in art and design from many of these notable craft workers and artists, so the goldwork produced at the school was of a very high standard both for church and ceremonial use.

Or Nué saw a revival in the early twentieth century and, although these were generally not large pieces of work, some were quite exquisite. The embroiderers of the twentieth century, like Beryl Dean, Jane Lemon and Barbara Dawson, have used metal threads in an imaginative and exciting way and those at the Royal School have the opportunity to undertake traditional techniques as well as modern commissions using not only the usual Japanese gold threads passing purls and twists, but some of the modern lurexes, working gold, silver and copper together in the same piece of work and adding manipulated metallic tissue fabric and leathers. Goldwork is a very exciting and underused technique. We hope the projects in this book will encourage you to try your hand at metal threads.

APPROACH TO GOLDWORK

Like all embroidery projects goldwork needs some thought and planning to achieve the best results. It must be remembered that some gold threads will slightly discolour with time, but this should not put an embroiderer off using them, as the whole effect will still be interesting many years ahead. Some of the cheap lurex threads are not always of good quality and their use could spoil the look of a finished project, so these types of thread should be selected with care.

If you are a beginner and metal threads are a new experience for you, be guided by the projects in this book. When you are familiar with the different types of thread, then you will feel happier about adding new ones to your collection and experimenting. Metal thread work should be undertaken with patience and a great deal of care. It is not possible to hurry this technique; even experienced goldworkers do not hurry their work.

One of the secrets of good metal thread work is the careful planning and preparation of the various areas to be worked. A good play of light on the gold thread can best be achieved when worked over padding. This can be layers of felt, carpet felt, string or soft embroidery cotton. Good padding will give a beautiful finish to your goldwork. The background fabric should be firm to prevent the work from puckering. It is a good idea to mount the background fabric on preshrunk cotton and always use a square frame (see page 10). Metal thread looks wonderful on most colours and fabrics, particularly silks and velvets. Patterned fabrics can detract from the embroidery. Space dyed silk is interesting and can look very rich and would give a modern feel to your project.

A design is not difficult to arrive at as most designs can be adapted to suit metal threads. The outline of the design should be cleanly drawn and areas left as uncomplicated as possible. Japanese gold and couched threads work well in flowing shapes, but purls need divided narrow areas. Choose a small design as an introduction to goldwork because this will be less daunting than a large project and will give you a chance to learn to handle the gold threads in a small way to start with. The design can be transferred on to the background by the prick and pounce method (see page 13) and the same pricking can be used to mark out the shapes of felt for padding.

Gold and metal threads come in different qualities. Japanese gold is 18 carat gold and is very expensive and difficult to find, but Imitation Japanese Gold thread is a very good substitute and will not tarnish. A second range of threads is known as Admiralty quality and these have a percentage of real gold, but are not as expensive as Japanese gold. The least expensive range of all is a gilt metallic thread. This looks similar to Admiralty gold and is fine for beginners to use but will tarnish more quickly.

Not only do gold threads fall into different qualities but also different types. The first group of threads is couched down with a gold or coloured beeswaxed couching thread. These are Japanese gold threads,

A crown from the Worshipful Company of Girdlers, worked by the Royal School of Needlework in 1946. This is an exact replica of a seventeenth-century piece, destroyed in the Blitz during the Second World War, reproduced by permission of the Worshipful Company of Girdlers.

passing, rococo, twists, plate and pearl purl. The second group of threads is purls cut into appropriate lengths and sewn down like beads over various methods of padding, and again a beeswaxed thread is used to protect against the rough gold threads.

It will be essential to use thimbles when working through all the thicknesses of padding, and fine needles will be needed to pass through the pure threads without damaging the gold thread. It is also a good idea to have a pair of scissors just for goldwork, as the gold can blunt your best embroidery scissors. However you will need a pair that will cut the gold cleanly. A mellor is a must for the serious goldworker. This is a wonderful little tool for turning and arranging your metal threads, and helps to prevent overhandling and tarnishing, but a pair of tweezers can also help if you take care not to damage the gold thread with the points. You should also make a cutting board to cut your purls on. This is a small square of card covered in velvet, the pile of the velvet helping

to stop the purls jumping about when they are being cut into lengths.

Goldwork is very much a textural form of embroidery and that is why it is important to combine a variety of threads in a project. Once you understand the texture, size and colour of each different thread you can introduce silver and copper threads too. These come in similar ranges of threads and the combinations can look stunning but they may tarnish slightly.

Once you have familiarized yourself with the potential of the various threads available, you will then be able to think about stitching in a free and creative way. Try combining metallic tissue fabrics, leathers and pieces of interesting textured fabrics in your projects. Some of the beautiful pearl lustre powders can be combined with a medium and painted on to leather or fabric and used in conjunction with gold threads, creating a beautiful subtle look. It is also possible to texture up a background fabric with the huge range of machine embroidery threads, with the finest of the machines lines complementing the heavier hand-embroidered metal threads.

Part-worked seventeenth-century embroidery showing leaves worked in coloured looped Purl threads, RSN Collection.

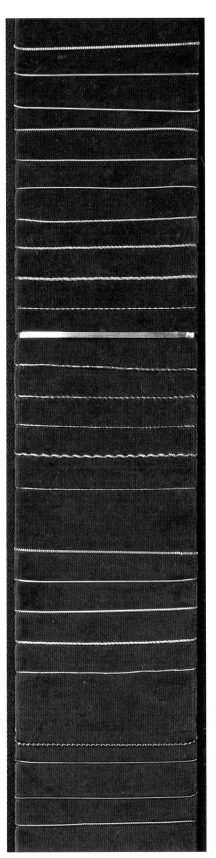

GOLD

Purls no. 6 Bright Check

no. 6 Smooth

no. 6 Rough
no. 1 Pearl Purl

Super Pearl Purl

very fine Pearl Purl

Twist no. 1 Twist

no. 1½ Twist

no. 3 Twist

Elizabethan Twist

no. 6 Broad Plate

Jap 13 (1K)

Jap 9 (3K)

Jap 8 (4K)

Medium Rococo

no. 5 Passing

SILVER

Purls no. 8 Bright Check

no. 8 Smooth

no. 1 Pearl Purl

Twist no. 1 Twist

no. 6 Passing

COPPER

Purls no. 8 Bright Check
no. 8 Smooth

no. 8 Rough

no. 1 Pearl Purl

EXERCISE FOR BEGINNERS

The Majolica tile design is again being used for an introduction to goldwork and should help build up confidence in handling gold threads if you have no previous experience. Simple padding with a good quality craft felt is used. Imitation Japanese thread no. 8 is couched to give a lovely play of light on the petal shapes, and the centre and corner shapes are worked in gold check purl no. 8 chips set in gold Pearl Purl no. 1. Gold twist no. 1½ neatens the edge of the petals.

Materials

- The background fabric is a cream slub silk which is herringboned on to preshrunk cotton, keeping the grain straight
- A 25 cm (10-inch) wide ring frame with 2.5 cm (1-inch) deep sides used in a floor stand or similar (you must have both hands free to manipulate the gold thread)
- One reel each no. 8 Imitation Japanese gold (4K) and Gütermann thread no. 488; 1 metre (38½ inches) each fine gold twist no. 1½ and fine gold Pearl Purl no. 1; a small quantity of gold Bright Check Purl no. 6; and a small square of good quality gold craft felt

Preparation

1 Tack a centre line on the background fabric both ways.
2 Draw the design accurately on to paper and, with the aid of a light box, trace the design with a hard pencil making sure the tacking on the background lines up with centre design lines (see page 15).
3 Mount the silk on to the preshrunk cotton with herringbone stitch.
4 Mount the background into a ring frame very tightly.
5 Tack the silk and backing cotton together with a small stab stitch just inside the paint line.
6 Pounce the padded areas of the design on to the felt.

The petal shapes will need three layers and the centre and corners one layer.

7 With a needle threaded with beeswaxed Gütermann thread, sew down the felt padding, starting with the smallest piece. For the final padding, come up on the paint line and sew down into the felt, working with small, fairly close stitches.

Instructions

1 Work gold Pearl Purl no. 1 around the edge of the corner shapes. Before stitching, open the twists in the Pearl Purl very slightly. Hold the very end of the Pearl Purl in the tips of your scissors and pull very slightly; this will make it easier for the couching stitches to slip down between the twists of the gold thread. Pearl Purl is not taken to the back of the work, so snip any damaged areas away so that the joins will butt together cleanly and will not show. Use a mellor to turn the corners neatly. Fill the centre of the corner shape with tiny gold Bright Check Purl chips. Cut these first on your velvet cutting board to the same width and length. Thread up each chip individually and sew on to the padded area, with as many different directions as possible, using a beeswaxed Gütermann thread.
2 Imitation Japanese gold no. 8 is couched down double with a beeswaxed Gütermann thread. Begin on the outside edge of the shape and work into the

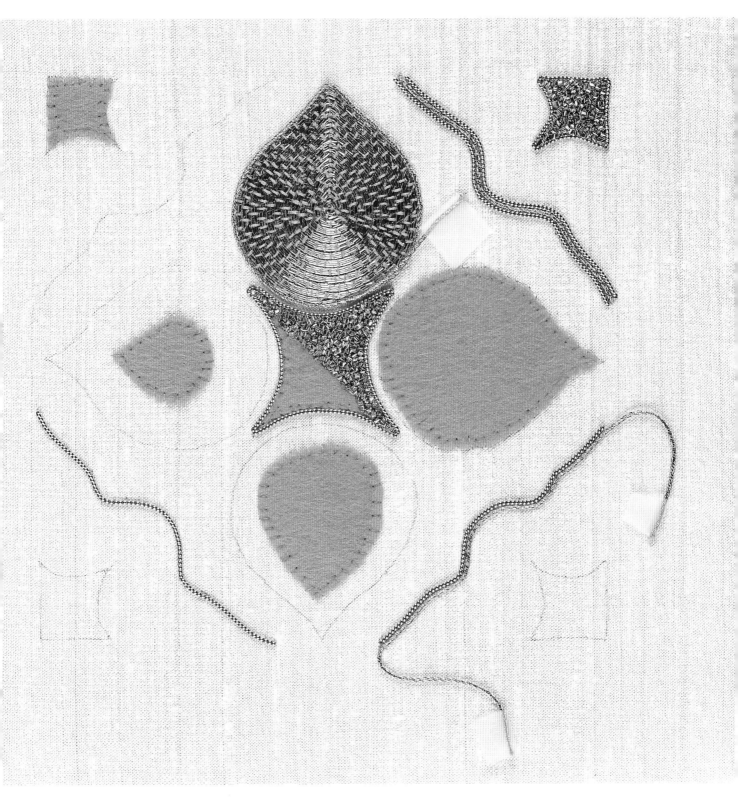

This small project shows the play of light on couched
Japanese gold and the rough texture of Bright Check chips
in the centre.

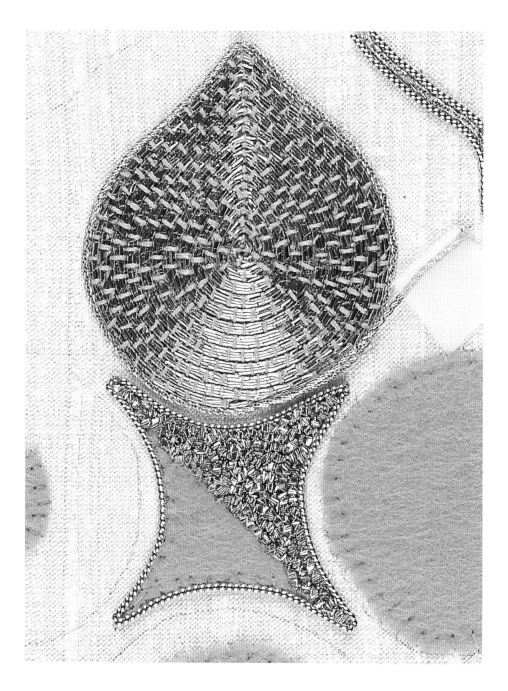

centre. The couching stitches are worked in a brick pattern (see page 154 Fig. 51). Reduce the numbers of stitches and adjust bricking as the area gets smaller. Take the ends of the gold thread down to the back of the work with a well beeswaxed lasso (see page 154 Fig. 53), sew back the ends and trim the excess.

3   Outline the petal shapes with gold fine twist no. 1½, using beeswaxed Gütermann thread and stitching into the twists of the gold thread so the couching

does not show. Plunge the ends of the Twist with a lasso or large needle and sew them back.

4   Work the centre of the design as the corner pieces (see step 1).

5   On the wavy lines, stitch gold fine Twist on the paint lines. Lasso the ends of the Twist and sew them back on the reverse of the work. Open up the twists of the Pearl Purl as in step 1 and sew down beside the fine Twist on both sides of the twist.

STITCH DIAGRAM

1 *One layer of padding, outline in Pearl Purl no. 1. Fill in with chips of gold Bright Check Purl no. 8*

2 *Three layers of padding, couch in bricking in Imitation Japanese gold no. 8*

3 *Outline in fine gold Twist no. 1½*

4 *One layer of padding (work as 1)*

5 *Work gold fine twist no. 1½ with no. 1 Pearl Purl each side*

ART NOUVEAU DESIGN

This little art nouveau motif has been chosen because it contains design areas suitable to work in basic goldwork techniques and will give a new goldworker shapes with the minimal amount of difficulties. Laid Imitation Japanese gold thread looks at its best when slightly padded and worked in shapes that twist and turn to give a wonderful play of light. However, purl threads work best in small design areas over padding. Remember that if threads are too long, they are liable to kink and buckle causing the gold to crack.

Materials

- A square peg frame mounted with preshrunk cotton backing
- Blue silk the size of the project plus mounting allowances
- A 10 cm (4-inch) square of yellow felt
- Crewel needles no. 10
- Imitation Japanese gold thread 4K or no. 8 (used double), gold Twist no. 1, gold Bright Check no. 6, gold Smooth Purl no. 6, gold Rough Purl no. 6, gold Pearl Purl no. 1, gold Super Pearl Purl and a reel of gold Gütermann thread no. 488

Preparation

1 Mount the blue silk on to your square frame (see page 12 method B).
2 Trace the design on to good quality tracing paper.
3 Prick and pounce and paint the design on to the blue silk (see page 13).

Instructions

Refer to the stitch plan and work the underneath shapes first.

1-10 This covers the areas of padding. Pounce these design areas on to your felt, pouncing twice where two layers of felt are needed. Cut out the felt on the pounce line. On the second layer of felt, trim just

Art Nouveau Design worked by Amanda Ewing.

inside the pounce line. Thread your needle with beeswaxed gold Gütermann no. 488. Sew down felt very carefully in the appropriate areas. Bring your needle up on the paint line and take it down into the felt, stitching closely and firmly as shown on the sampler on page 131. Remember, good padding is essential to good goldwork. Use beeswaxed Gütermann no. 488 throughout.

11-12 Imitation Japanese gold thread no. 13 is couched double on the leaves, bricking the stitches on each row (see Fig.51, page 154). Plunge the ends of the gold thread and sew them back on to the worked leaves on the back of the embroidery, then outline in no. 1 Pearl Purl.

13-14 The two base leaves are now worked in no. 13 Imitation Japanese gold. Plunge the ends and sew them back, then outline in no. 1½ gold Twist.

15-16 The flower stems are worked in Twist no. 1½ which is sewn down the centre (see Fig. 62, page 155) and outlined down each side in Super Pearl Purl (see Fig. 61, page 155).

17-18 The four top petals of the top flower are outlined in Super Pearl Purl and the centre is satin stitched in no. 6 Smooth gold Purl (see page 156).

19-20 The stamen stems are worked in Super Pearl Purl, and no. 6 Bright Check chips fill in the tops.

21-22 The base of the petal with a turnover edge is outlined in Super Pearl Purl and infilled with satin stitch using no. 6 Rough Purl (see page 156).

23-24 The turnover is outlined with Super Pearl Purl and infilled with no. 6 Bright Check chips (see page 156).

25-26 The left-hand petal of the lower flower is outlined in Super Pearl Purl and satin stitched in no. 6 Rough Purl.

27-28 The two right-hand petals are outlined in Super Pearl Purl and infilled with no. 6 Bright Check chips.

29-30 The base of the flower is outlined in Super Pearl Purl and satin stitched in no. 6 Smooth Purl.

31 The spots at the base of flower stems are satin stitched in no. 6 Smooth Purl.

STITCH DIAGRAM

1–10 Felt areas 1, 2, 5, 6, 8, 9, 10, one layer. Felt areas 3, 4, 7, two layers

11–12 Imitation Japanese gold no. 13, couched with Gütermann 488, outlined in no. 1 Pearl Purl

13–14 Imitation Japanese gold no. 13, outline in 1½ gold Twist

15–16 Twist no. 1½, outlined in Super Pearl Purl

17–18 Outline in Super Pearl Purl, satin stitch in no. 6 Smooth gold Purl

19–20 Super Pearl Purl stamens with no. 6 Bright Check chips

21–22 Outline in Super Pearl Purl satin stitch in no. 6 Rough Purl

23–24 Outline in Super Pearl Purl, infill in Bright Check no. 6 chips

25–26 Outline in Super Pearl Purl, infill with satin stitch in no. 6 Rough Purl

27–28 Outline in Super Pearl Purl, infill with no. 6 Bright Check chips

29–30 Outline in Super Pearl Purl, satin stitch in no. 6 Smooth Purl

31 Satin stitch in no. 6 Smooth Purl

IRIS

The fourth and final use of an iris as a design source has been interpreted with less detail to take into account the goldwork techniques to be covered in this section. These will include a variation of *Or Nué* and burden stitch as well as padding with soft cotton string known as bump. The design also includes some painted areas.

Materials

- A square peg frame dressed with preshrunk cotton
- A piece of cream silk. Tack the centre line
- Red and green silk, which could be white silk dyed with silk dyes
- A small square of good quality yellow felt for the padded areas of the design, both gold and silk
- Crewel needles nos. 10-12
- DMC soft embroidery thread no. 2725 (for padding); DMC stranded cotton no. 350; Anchor stranded cotton nos. 323, 324, 39, 59, 43 214, 216 and 217; a reel of Gütermann gold no. 488; gold Passing no. 5 (used double); gold Twist no. 1; gold Rococo medium; gold Super Pearl Purl and gold very fine Pearl Purl (grip the end of the Pearl Purls with scissors and pull to open twists very slightly to allow stitches to sink into the thread); gold Imitation Japanese gold 3K or no. 9 (used double); gold Rough Purl no. 8; gold Smooth Purl no. 8; and gold Bright Check no. 8

Preparation

1 Draw your design on to good quality tracing paper. Mark a centre line both ways.
2 Mount the cream background silk. Prick, pounce and paint the design on to the already prepared frame (see page 13), matching the centre lines.
3 Paint the design lines with a fine paint line.
4 Pounce and paint the design on to the red and green silk, matching the grain on the background, petals on red and leaves on green.

(Above) Silk fabric painted, ready to be worked
(Right) Finished piece worked by Tracy Franklin

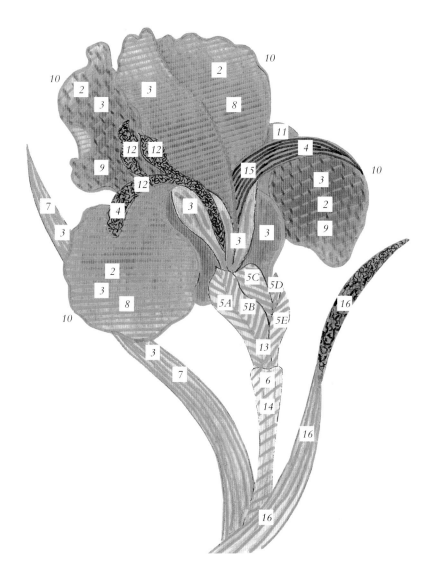

STITCH DIAGRAM

1 *Pounce design onto felt with appropriate design areas*

2 *Padding: top and bottom right petals one layer, bottom left one layer, turnover one layer*

3 *Apply red and green silk to petals and left leaf*

4 *Sew another layer of felt on stamen areas*

5 *Calix pad with soft cotton, 5A, 5C, 5D use 8 strands, 5B 10 strands, 5E 4 strands*

6 *Pad stem with 20 strands of soft cotton*

7 *On leaf on left couch Imitation Japanese gold 3K (9) with Anchor stranded cotton nos. 214, 216, 217, outline in Super Pearl Purl*

8 *Or Nué worked over 3K (9) Imitation Japanese gold couched in DMC 350 and Anchor 43, 59, 39, 324, 323*

9 *Burden stitch no. 5 gold Passing, worked over in DMC 350, Anchor 43, 59, 39, 324, 323*

10 *Outline in Super Pearl Purl*

11 *Left turnover Smooth Purl no. 8, right hand small area Rough Purl no. 8*

12 *Bright Check Purl no. 8 chips in stamen area, outline Super Pearl Purl*

13 *Calyx: 5A 5B 5E worked in Smooth Purl no. 8, 5C 5D worked in Rough Purl no. 8*

14 *Stem worked in cut work in Smooth Purl no. 8 and Rough Purl no. 8*

15 *Work alternating rows of no. 1 gold Twist and medium Rococo outline in Super Pearl Purl*

16 *Apply green fabric on right-hand leaf work veins as no. 7, outline in Super Pearl Purl and infill turnover with Bright Check no. 8 chips*

Instructions

Use a beeswaxed Gütermann or appropriate couching thread throughout.

1   Pounce the felt with the design areas to be padded and cut out accurately.

2   The left-hand leaf is not padded. Pad the right-hand leaf with one layer. The bottom left petal has one layer of padding, the top left has no padding and there is one layer turnover. The top right has two layers of felt, the bottom right one layer. Where two layers of felt are needed, pounce felt twice. Trim the second layer of felt inside the pounce line and sew this down first. No padding is used in the plain red and green areas. Stitch the felt down carefully with small stitches, bringing the needle up on the paint line and down into the felt.

3   Pounce and paint the design on to the red and green silk, cut out just outside the paint line and sew down over the felt with small oversewing stitches. Stab stitch between the petals.

4   Sew another layer of felt on the stamen areas and on the leaf turnover.

5   The calyx is padded with beeswaxed soft cotton, sewn with beeswaxed Gütermann thread chamfered off at the points.

5a 8 strands of soft cotton

5b 10 strands of soft cotton

5c Two rows of 8 strands of soft cotton

5e 4 strands of soft cotton

5d 8 strands of soft cotton

6   Pad the stem with 20 strands of beeswaxed soft cotton.

7   Work the vein lines in couched Imitation Japanese gold 3K or no. 9. Couch with three shades of Anchor stranded cotton nos. 214, 216 and 217. Outline the left-hand one only with Super Pearl Purl. Now work the four main petals.

8   The bottom left and top right petals are worked in.

Graduated *Or Nué* coloured threads are couched over 3K or no. 9 Imitation Japanese gold. The lines of gold are wide at the top of the petal and close at the base. Couch in one strand of beeswaxed stranded cotton in the following shades: Anchor nos. 43, 59 and 39; DMC no. 350; and Anchor nos. 324 and 323 (see Stitch Diagram). The couching stitches are spaced out at the top of the petal and the stitches get closer together as the work progresses to the base. At the base the stitches are completely solid, with no gold thread visible.

9   The top left and bottom right petals are worked in burden stitch, working over double laid no. 5 gold Passing evenly spaced. The burden stitches are worked in the same shades as the *Or Nué* (see Stitch Diagram).

10 When the burden stitch and *Or Nué* areas are completed, outline the petals with Super gold Pearl Purl.

11 The left-hand petal turnover is worked in no. 8 Smooth Purl and the right is worked in Rough Purl no. 8.

12 The stamen area has a cutwork outline in Super Pearl and is worked in no. 8 Bright Check chips.

13 Work small calyxes in slanting satin stitch in gold purls as follows: outline in Super Pearl Purl – 5A, 5B, and 5E are worked in Smooth Purl no. 8 cutwork; 5C and 5D are worked in Rough Purl no. 8 cutwork.

14 The stem is worked in slanting cutwork in Smooth no. 8 at the top and Rough Purl no. 8 at the base.

15 The gold turned-over edge of the petals on the right is worked in alternating rows of no. 1 gold Twist and medium Rococo, outlined in Super Pearl Purl.

16 Apply green fabric. Work veins as no. 7 on right leaf. Now outline the right turned-over leaf in Super Pearl Purl and infill the turnover in gold no. 8 Bright Check chips.

SAMPLER

The origins of this sampler design came from a linen sampler owned by the Royal School and dated 1771. The shapes included in the design lend themselves to the various techniques to be used in this more advanced piece of goldwork. Old textiles and embroideries can be a good source of design ideas, but it is never good to copy contemporary embroiderers' ideas; they have put a great deal of hard work into their embroidery and have taken it as far as it is reasonable to go.

Goldwork is very much a textural technique and when choosing a design you have to consider the shapes very carefully to give the best possible results. This project should give you more insight into the various possibilities of the goldwork techniques which have been included, mixing copper and gold threads. The central flower has a reversed form of padding, using the largest piece of felt on the bottom of the flower working up to the smallest on the top, giving a crisp edge to the design. We have also used Broad Plate, cut gold and copper over string, couched Twist and the technique known as S-ing in some elements of the design.

Materials

- A square peg frame dressed with preshrunk cotton
- Silk for the background in your own choice of colour. Tack the centre lines
- A square of gold felt
- Fine beeswaxed string, 10 cm (4 inches) long
- Two 5 cm (2-inch) squares Bondaweb
- Crewel needles nos. 10-12
- Large needle for plunging threads
- DMC soft embroidery thread no. 2725, for padding; 1 reel of gold Gütermann thread no. 488; gold twist nos. 1½ and 3, and Elizabethan Twist; Super gold Pearl Purl and gold Pearl Purl and copper Pearl Purl no. 1; Bright Check copper and gold Purl no. 8; Smooth Purl copper and gold no. 8; Rough Purl copper and gold no. 8; Imitation Japanese gold no. 8; Broad Plate gold no. 6; Anchor stranded cotton no. 561; and Madeira metallic copper no. 40

Preparation

1 Draw the design on to good quality tracing paper. Mark centre lines both ways.

2 Mount the coloured silk on to your square frame.

3 Prick and pounce on to the background (page 13).

4 Paint the design on to the background with a very fine line (see page 14).

Instructions

Use beeswaxed Gütermann thread or appropriate couching thread throughout. See points 1-12 on page 135 for the padding used, and points 13-48 on page 136 for numbering the type of gold thread and the techniques. Work the underneath pieces first.

1-12 Layers of felt are used on nos. 1, 5, 6, 7 and 10: 1 is worked with the largest padding first, working to the smallest, giving a crisp edge to the shape; 8 and 9 are

(Above) Part worked design showing padded areas

padded with beeswaxed soft cotton sewn down and chamfered off at the point; 11 is padded with fine string well sewn down with the space between the width of the string; in 12, Bondaweb a piece of felt on to a piece of background silk. Refer to the goldwork padding techniques on pages 157M and 158.

13 With the acorn, stitch no. 3 gold Twist down the middle of the stem, a row of no. 1 Pearl Purl either side, and gold Super Pearl Purl on the outside.

14 For the acorn and flower stem, work no. 3 gold Twist down the centre then alternating rows of no. 8 Japanese gold and 1½ gold Twist.

15 The side main stems are worked in a slanting cutwork stitch using Rough copper and gold no. 8. Start at the base with the copper, gradually working up the stem into gold.

16 The acorns are in gold Broad Plate no. 6 (see Stitch Diagram, page 155, Figs. 60a, 60b). Start at the top and work down to the cup. Be careful; plate is fragile.

17 The top of the acorn is finished off with a looped chip in no. 8 Smooth copper Purl.

18 The acorn cup is worked in S-ing starting under the plate in alternate rows of copper and gold Bright Check No. 8 (see Figs. 57, 58, page 155).

19 The small daisy flower is worked in Imitation Japanese gold thread no. 8. Starting on the outside working in, use alternate rows of Anchor stranded cotton no. 561 and Gütermann thread no. 488 using one strand beeswaxed.

20 Outline the centre and petals in gold Super Pearl Purl.

21 The centre is filled with tiny chips in no. 8 Bright Check copper.

22 Use Elizabethan Twist double and work one section at a time, working out from the centre. Couch on the outside across the shape, stitching on the three inside lines. When you reach the outside edge, couch down the inside length of Twist on the line and then the outside. The couching thread is Anchor stranded cotton no. 561 beeswaxed.

23 The leaves on the bottom flowers are worked in gold Smooth Purl cutwork with a S-ing vein in Bright Check no. 8.

24 The top of this flower is worked in cutwork over string. The string is sewn down firmly first with the width of string between each row. Start in the centre and stitch pieces of Smooth Purl gold no. 8 over every two pieces of string. Repeat this row. The third and fourth row are worked dropping down one string, and the fifth and sixth row are the same as the first and second. This gives a basket effect. Work half stitches to complete the shape.

25 The petals are worked in no. 8 Japanese gold thread, couched down with one strand of Anchor stranded cotton no. 561, working from the outside in.

26-27 These leaves are worked in cutwork using copper Smooth and Bright Check Purl alternately. The S-ing veins are worked in gold Smooth Purl no. 8 and gold Bright Check.

28 This leaf is worked as the previous two but using gold Smooth Purl no. 8 and gold Bright Check no. 8. The S-ing vein is Smooth Purl copper no. 8.

29 The flower stem is worked in cut gold and copper Rough Purl no. 8 with the stitches at right angles to the stem. Work gold at the top to copper at the base.

Sampler worked by Amanda Ewing.

30 The calyx is worked in gold Smooth and Rough Purl no. 8, working from the point in smooth to the base in rough. The veins are worked in overstretched copper Pearl Purl no. 1.

31 Large petals are couched in two rows of Imitation Japanese gold no. 8 and one row of copper Pearl Purl no. 1 alternately, working from the outside in.

32 Outline the petals in Super Pearl Purl gold and infill the centres with gold and copper Bright Check no. 8 chips.

33 Outline the petals with gold Pearl Purl no. 1. Work cut gold in the centre in gold Bright Check and Smooth Purl no. 8, working one Bright Check and two smooth alternately and starting in the centre and working out.

34 Outline the circle with 1½ gold twist using Gütermann thread no. 488. Work up to where the chips will be looped.

35 Outline the centre in gold Super Pearl Purl.

36 Loop tiny copper Smooth Purl chips no. 8 between 34 and 35. These should be tiny loops.

37 The flower centre is filled with copper Bright Check chips no. 8.

38-39 These tendrils are worked in gold Pearl Purl no. 1 and Super Pearl Purl.

40 Couched 1½ gold twist is worked here, from the outside point to the centre using Gütermann thread no. 488 in the needle.

41 The eyelets are worked in one strand of Anchor stranded cotton no. 561.

42 For the border, the corner eyelets are worked in copper machine thread no. 40 Madeira.

43 In the centre, eyelets worked in tiny gold Smooth Purl no. 8 chips. Stitch the loops horizontally and vertically alternately.

44 Eyelets outlined in couched Imitation Japanese gold no. 8 using two strands of Madeira copper machine thread no. 40.

Felt padding plan

STITCH DIAGRAM

1 *1st layer to be sewn down*

2nd

3rd

4th

5th

5 layers of felt

2 *10 pieces of soft cotton*

3 *10 pieces of soft cotton*

4 *10 pieces of soft cotton sewn down layer of felt sewn over the top of soft cotton*

5 *4 layers to be sewn down, starting with smallest size*

6 *1st layer of felt*

2nd

3rd

Back stitch on dotted line

7 *One piece of felt in each petal*
Large piece of felt in flower shape stitched over the small pieces

8 *5 pieces of soft cotton for each side of leaf. Start in centre and cut away towards the points*

9 *6 pieces of soft cotton for each side of the leaf work as no. 8*

10 *1st smaller layer of felt to sew down*
2nd larger one to follow

11 *Sew down rows of string*

12 *Bondaweb 1 piece of felt to a piece of background fabric this shape. Cut out and stitch down*

13 *Acorn stem, in centre gold Twist no. 3, either side gold Pearl Purl no. 1, outside line stitch Super Pearl Purl*

14 *Stem, centre gold Twist no. 3, either side gold Imitation Japanese gold no. 8, then two rows of gold Twist no. 1½*

15 *Stem in cutwork in gold and copper Rough Purl no. 8*

16 *Acorns worked in gold Broad Plate no. 6*

17 *Tip of acorn worked in Smooth Purl copper no. 8*

18 *Acorn cup in rows of gold/copper Bright Check no. 8 S-ing*

19 *Couched Imitation Japanese gold no. 8 using a stranded cotton 561, Gutemann 488 alternate rows*

20 *Outline centre in gold Super Pearl Purl, and petals*

21 *Centre of flower worked in copper Bright Check chips no. 8*

22 *Couch Elizabethan gold Twist with Anchor 561*

23 *Satin stitch leaves in gold Smooth Purl no. 8, with S-ing vein of gold Bright Check no. 8*

24 *Cut work over string in gold Smooth Purl no. 8*

25 *Couched Imitation Japanese gold no. 8 in Anchor stranded cotton no. 561*

26-27 *These leaves are worked in cut work using copper Smooth Bright Check Purl, alternatively the veins are worked in gold Smooth Purl no. 8 S-ing and bright gold check*

28 *Cut work leaf in gold Smooth/Bright Check Purl no. 8. Vein in copper Smooth Purl no. 8 S-ing*

29 *Cut work flower stem in gold and copper Rough Purl no. 8*

30 *Calyx worked in cut gold Smooth/Rough Purl no. 8 with vein of over stretched copper Pearl Purl*

31 *Large petals couched in Imitation Japanese gold no. 8 and copper Pearl Purl no. 1*

32 *Outline petals with gold Super Pearl Purl and fill centres with gold/copper Bright Check no. 8 chips*

33 *Outline petals with gold Pearl Purl no. 1 cut gold in centre with gold Bright Check and Smooth Purl no. 8*

34 *Outline circle with Gold Twist no. 1½*

35 *Outline centre in gold Super Pearl Purl*

36 *Looped chips of copper Smooth Purl no. 8 between nos. 34 and 35*

37 *Flower centre worked in chips of copper Bright Check no. 8*

38-39 *Work in gold Pearl Purl no. 1 and Super Pearl Purl*

40 *Couched gold Twist no. 1½*
Border:

41 *Eyelet worded in one strand of Anchor stranded no. 561*

42 *Corner eyelets worked in copper machine thread no. 40 Madeira*

43 *In centre of border, eyelets worked in good Smooth no. 8 looped chips*

Stitch plan

PURSE

For our final more advanced project we have returned to architecture for our design source. An archway in Durham Cathedral gives us the shapes that are suitable for goldwork. This project will cover the use of carpet felt to give very raised areas and it will incorporate manipulated metallic tissue. Silver and gold threads are used and include the use of overstretched Pearl Purl with a coloured thread running through it and then sewn down.

As with all goldwork techniques, a great deal of care must be taken when applying the felt and other paddings. They must be exactly the shape of the painted design lines. Take great care when painting the design on to the felt and background fabric.

Materials
- Metallic tissue or similar fabric and metallic thread to match
- A square peg frame dressed with preshrunk calico. Mark the centre
- A small square of carpet felt and a square of good quality gold and white craft felt
- Crewel needles nos. 10-12
- Large needle for plunging or lassoing gold threads to the back of the work where they are sewn back
- Anchor stranded cotton nos. 146 and 19; gold and grey Gütermann thread; silver smooth Passing no. 6; gold and silver Bright Check no. 8; gold and silver Pearl Purl no. 1; gold and silver Smooth Purl no. 8; gold and silver twist no. 1½; gold very fine Pearl Purl; gold Broad Plate no. 6; and DMC soft embroidery thread no. 2727, for the padding

Preparation
1 Draw the design very accurately on to good quality tracing paper, marking the centre lines both ways. As this project is worked in solid metal threads and manipulated fabric, no background is needed.
2 Match the centre lines and prick and pounce the design on to the calico on the dressed frame.
3 Paint the design with fine accurate lines (see page 14).
4 Pounce the areas of the design to be padded on to the yellow and white felt and carpet felt, then paint carefully. Where two layers of felt are required, pounce extra shapes.

Instructions
Refer to the Padding Chart (points 1-11) and to the Stitch Diagram (points 12-34). Use beeswaxed thread throughout and plunge and sew back the ends as the work progresses.

1 Apply areas of manipulated fabric to the design, using tiny stab stitches to hold the fabric as you manipulate it and using a matching fine metallic thread in the needle. Take the fabric a fraction over the adjoining paint lines and trim.
2 Apply half a layer of carpet felt to this central area, chamfering the edges, and stitch down carefully (see page 158).
3 Apply a layer of white felt over this carpet felt.

Purse worked by Amanda Ewing.

4 Apply half a layer of carpet felt to these side leaf shapes, chamfering the edges, and stitch well.

5 Cover the felt leaves with one layer of yellow felt.

6 Cover the small round areas down the centre pad with one layer of yellow felt.

7 Pad the half circle areas on the right and left with one layer of white felt.

8 Cover the two shapes at the base with one layer of white felt.

9 Cover the ten tiny petal shapes with one layer of yellow felt.

10 Pad the four outside leaf shapes with four lengths of soft cotton, beeswaxed, each side of the vein, chamfering off at the points (see page 158).

11 Cover with one layer of white felt. (Refer to second chart).

12 The basic padding is now complete. Now add extra layers to give an even more sculptured look to the design. Add one layer of yellow felt to the centre.

13 Add one layer of white felt to the four eye-shaped pattern areas.

14 Stitch one layer of yellow felt to two central leaf shapes.

15 Stitch two layers of yellow felt to right and left circle.

16 Add one more layer of yellow felt to the areas above and below the circles.

17 The padding is now completed and the metal thread work can begin, working underneath shapes first. Satin stitch in Anchor stranded cotton no. 146.

18 Work in cut silver Bright Check Purl no. 8.

19 Use overstretched gold Pearl Purl no. 1 with Anchor stranded cotton no. 19 in the centre.

20 Cutwork in silver Bright Check Purl no. 8.

21 *Or Nué* is worked over silver Passing no. 6. The couching thread is Anchor stranded cotton no. 146. The centre is stitched with no silver visible. Refer to the photograph for the points.

22 This is worked in gold Smooth Purl no. 8 outlined in gold Pearl Purl no. 1.

23 Outline the centre with gold Pearl Purl no. 1.

24 Fill the centre with gold Bright Check chips no. 8.

25 Work the outer centre outline in silver Pearl Purl

no. 1 overstretched and sewn with Anchor stranded cotton no. 19.

26 Infill between 25 and 23 with silver Bright Check chips no. 8.

27 Work in gold Broad Plate no. 6

28 These four leaf shapes are worked in alternating stitches of silver Pearl Purl no. 1 and gold twist 1½.

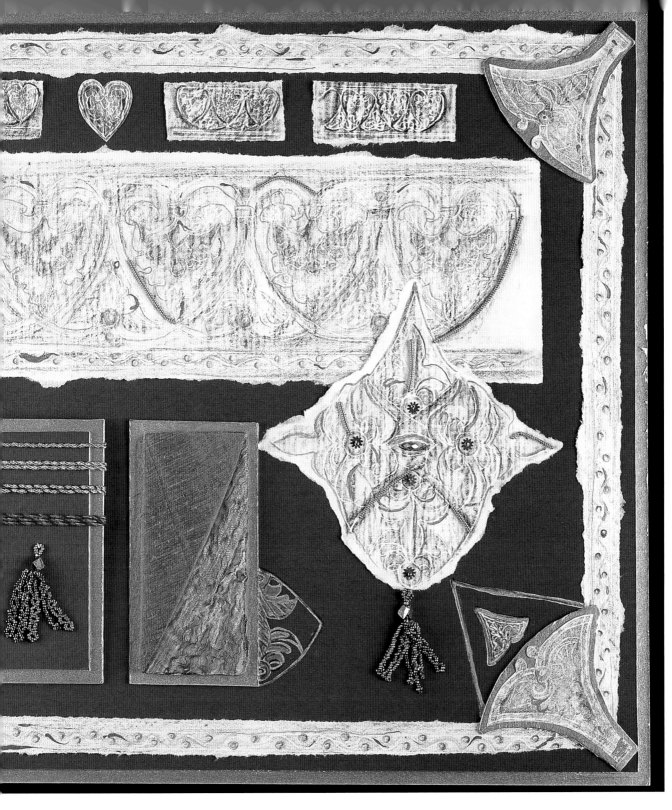

29 The 14 tiny petal shapes are outlined in gold very fine Pearl Purl.

30 Infill the petal shapes with gold Bright Check chips no. 8.

31 The four outside leaf shapes are worked in slanting stitches in gold Smooth Purl no. 8 and silver Smooth Purl no. 8, stitched alternately.

32 The veins in the four leaves are worked in gold Pearl Purl no. 1.

33 Overstretched gold Pearl Purl no. 1 couched with Anchor stranded cotton no. 19.

34 The blue *Or Nué* area is neatened with silver twist no. 1½. This is stitched down into the twists so the stitches are invisible.

PADDING CHART

1   *Fabric manipulation using metallic tissue*
2   *Half layer of carpet felt*
3   *One layer of white felt*
4   *Half layer of carpet felt*
5   *One layer of yellow felt*
6   *One layer of yellow felt*
7   *One layer of white felt*
8   *One layer of white felt*
9   *One layer of yellow felt*
10 *Four lengths of soft cotton*
11 *One layer of white felt*

STITCH DIAGRAM

Extra layers of felt:
12 *One layer of yellow felt*
13 *One layer of white felt*
14 *One layer of yellow felt*
15 *Two layers of yellow felt*
16 *One layer of yellow felt*
17 *Satin stitch in Anchor no. 146*
18 *Cutwork in silver Bright Check no. 8*
19 *Overstretched gold Pearl Purl no. 1 couched down with Anchor stranded cotton no.19*
20 *Cut silver Bright Check no. 8*
21 *Or Nué over silver smooth passing no. 6 working with Anchor 16*
22 *Cut gold Smooth Purl no. 8, outlined in Pearl Purl no. 1*
23 *Outline in gold Pearl Purl no. 1*
24 *Chipwork in gold Bright Check no. 8*
25 *Outline in no. 1 silver Pearl Purl using Anchor stranded cotton no. 19*
26 *Chipwork in silver Bright Check no. 8*
27 *Gold Broad Plate no. 6*
28 *Alternate rows of silver Pearl Purl no. 1 and gold Twist 1½*
29 *Outline in very fine gold Pearl Purl*
30 *Fill with gold Bright Check chips no. 9*
31 *Cutwork gold Smooth Purl no. 8 and silver Smooth Purl no. 8*
32 *Veins in gold Pearl Purl no. 1*
33 *Overstretched gold Pearl Purl no. 1, couched with Anchor stranded cotton no. 19*
34 *Silver twist no. 1½*

STITCH GLOSSARY

Crewel work stitches can be used for any surface embroidery. A number of stitches can be used to add texture and interest to a piece. Below are the stitches used on the projects in the crewel work section.

Fig.1 *Seeding stitches (approximately 1 mm (¹⁄₁₆ in) in length)*

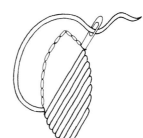

Fig.4 *Satin stitch worked over split stitch edge.*

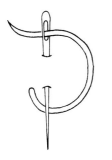

Fig.2a *Buttonhole stitch (1st stage)*

Fig.5a *Bullion knots (1st stage)*

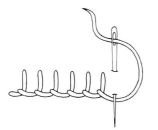

Fig.2b *Buttonhole stitch (2nd stage)*

Fig.5b *Bullion knots (2nd stage)*

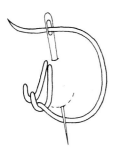

Fig.3 *Closed buttonhole stitch*

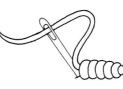

Fig.5c *Bullion knots (3rd stage)*

Fig.6a *French knot (1st stage)*

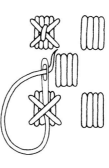

Fig.8 *Chequered filling*

Fig.6b *French knot (2nd stage)*

Fig.9 *Running stitch*

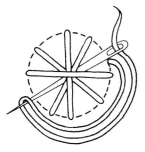

Fig.7a *Whipped spider's web (1st stage) – the spokes are knotted together with the last spoke.*

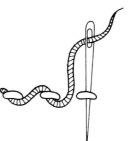

Fig.10 *Threaded running stitch*

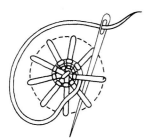

Fig.7b *Whipped spider's web (2nd stage) – work back over one spoke and forward under two.*

Fig.11 *Pekinese stitch*

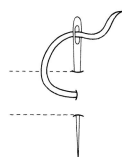

Fig.12a *Knotted pearl stitch (1st stage)*

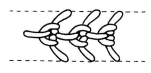

Fig.12e *Knotted pearl stitch (5th stage)*

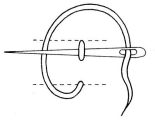

Fig.12b *Knotted pearl stitch (2nd stage)*

Fig.12f *Knotted pearl stitch (6th stage)*

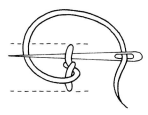

Fig.12c *Knotted pearl stitch (3rd stage)*

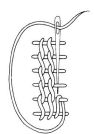

Fig.13 *Raised stem band*

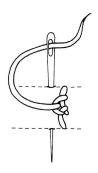

Fig.12d *Knotted pearl stitch (4th stage)*

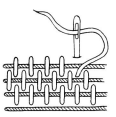

Fig.14 *Burden stitch*

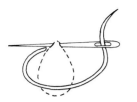

Fig. 15a *Vandyke stitch (1st stage)*

Fig. 17a *Cretan stitch (1st stage)*

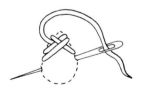

Fig. 15b *Vandyke stitch (2nd stage) – take the needle under the previous stitch*

Fig. 17b *Cretan stitch (2nd stage)*

Fig. 16a *Vandyke stitch (3rd stage)*

Fig. 17c *Cretan stitch (3rd stage)*

Fig. 16b *Vandyke stitch (4th stage)*

Fig. 17d *Cretan stitch (4th stage)*

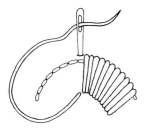

Fig.18a *Block shading (1st stage) – work a band of satin stitch over split stitch.*

Fig. 21 *Twisted chain stitch*

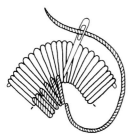

Fig.18b *Block shading (2nd stage) – take the needle down between stitches on the first row.*

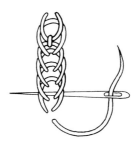

Fig.22 *Heavy chain stitch*

Fig.18c *Block shading (3rd stage)*

Fig.23 *Open chain stitch*

Fig.19 *Whipped chain stitch*

Fig.24 *Split stitch*

Fig 20 *Chain stitch*

Fig.25 *Wave stitch*

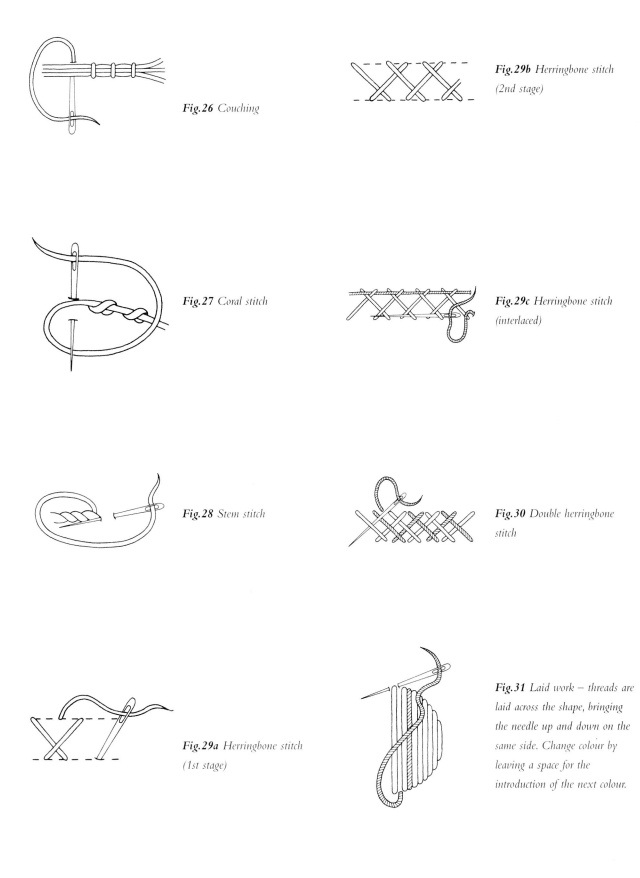

Fig.26 Couching

Fig.29b Herringbone stitch
(2nd stage)

Fig.27 Coral stitch

Fig.29c Herringbone stitch
(interlaced)

Fig.28 Stem stitch

Fig.30 Double herringbone
stitch

Fig.29a Herringbone stitch
(1st stage)

Fig.31 Laid work – threads are
laid across the shape, bringing
the needle up and down on the
same side. Change colour by
leaving a space for the
introduction of the next colour.

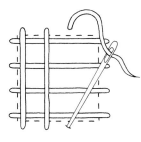

Fig.32 *Square filling – basic (variation 1) with laid threads.*

Fig.37 *Square filling decorated using weaving.*

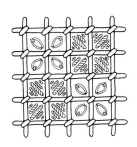

Fig.33 *Square filling – basic (variation 2), laid threads held in place with small half cross stitches.*

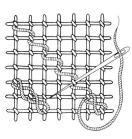

Fig.38 *Square filling decorated using lacing.*

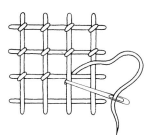

Fig.34 *Square filling decorated using detached chain.*

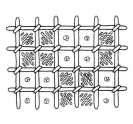

Fig.39 *Square filling decorated with French knots and satin stitch squares.*

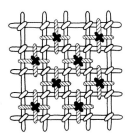

Fig.35 *Square filling decorated using cross stitch.*

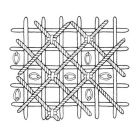

Fig.40 *Overlaid square filling with detached chain stitches.*

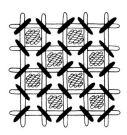

Fig.36 *Square filling decorated using satin stitch.*

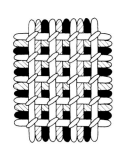

Fig.41 *Square filling overlaid in three colours.*

Blackwork is based on individual geometric shapes which are built up to form a continuous pattern. The following pages show how patterns can be constructed from their simplest forms to completed designs.

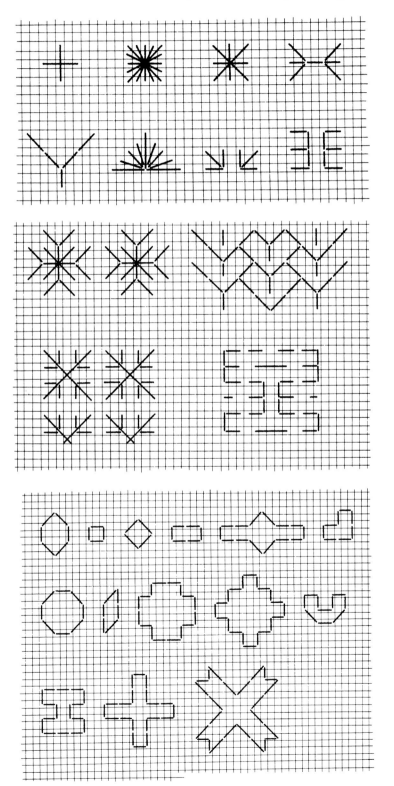

Fig.42 Basic pointed blackwork patterns made with straight stitches.

Fig.43 Compound patterns made with straight stitches.

Fig.44 Basic geometric shapes

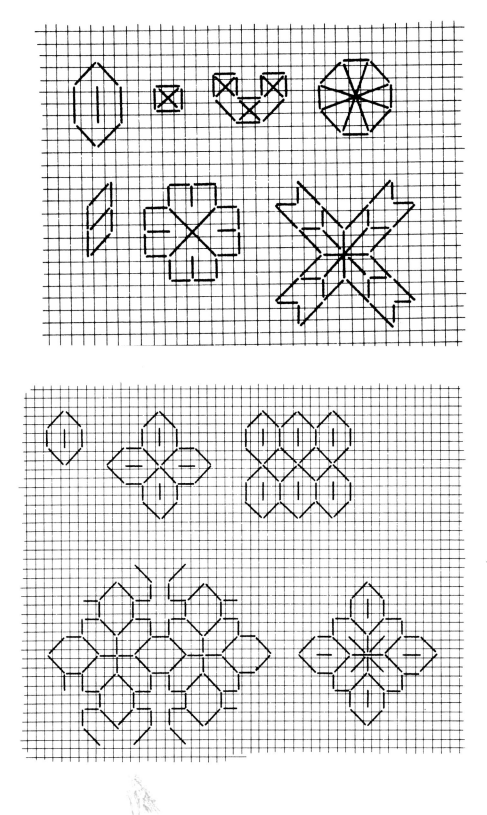

Fig.45 *Basic geometric shapes decorated with extra stitches.*

Fig.46 *One geometric shape is joined to another, altering the angle of the shapes.*

Fig. 47 *The basic pattern is in the centre of each block. Stitches are increased to darken the pattern at the base and stitches are omitted to lighten the pattern at the top.*

Goldwork is a very textural form of embroidery, so it is important to combine different techniques – for both stitching and padding – in the design. Below are the most widely used techniques for goldwork.

Fig. 48 Couched gold threads with even stitches.

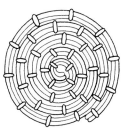

Fig. 52 Working a circle outside to centre. (See page 156B)

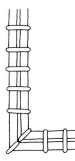

Fig. 49 Couched gold threads with a right-angled corner. (See page 156A)

Fig. 53 Plunge ends of gold thread with large needle, or lasso of thread in a needle (a lasso is a short length of waxed thread taken through the needle twice, providing a large soft loop that does not damage the gold threads).

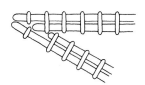

Fig. 50 Couched gold threads with an acute corner. (See page 156C)

Fig. 54 Purl gold threads sewn over padding as satin stitch. (See page 156D, 156F)

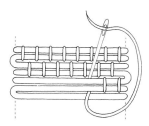

Fig. 51 Turning laid gold and bricking laid stitches.

Fig. 55 Purls cut into tiny chips and stitched randomly.

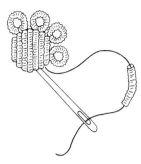

Fig.56 *Length of purl (cut just long enough to double over) is sewn down to give a raised petal shape of gold.*

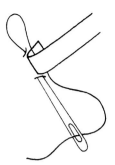

Fig.60a *Plate application (stage 1) Make a fold in plate and use this to secure plate at the start and finish.*
(See page 157G)

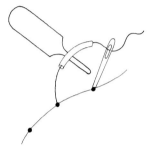

Fig.57 *S-ing for stems, using a mellor for positioning the gold threads.*

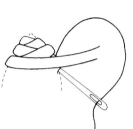

Fig.60b *Plate application (stage 2) Work across shape with plate turn, stitching each side of shape. (See page 157 H)*

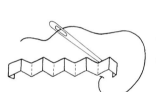

Fig.60c *Plate application – the plate can be indented on a wood screw and sewn down.*

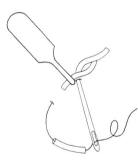

Fig.58 *S-ing for veins*

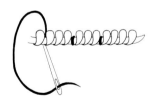

Fig.61 *Couching Pearl Purl (stage 1), the Pearl Purl is shown outstretched so the stitches can be seen. When actually worked, the stitches should be invisible.*
(See page 157K)

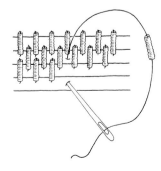

Fig.59 *Burden stitch – parallel lines of any thread are laid down first and purls are bricked over them.*

Fig.62 *Twist is sewn down by stitching into the twist at the same angle as the cord twists, so the stitches are unseen.*
(See page 157L)

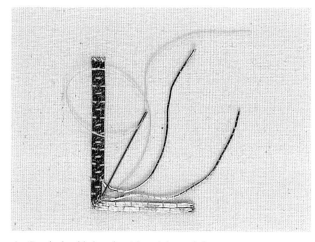

A *Couched gold threads with a right angled corner.*

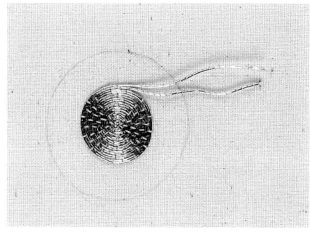

B *This is the only shape that can be worked from the centre out.*

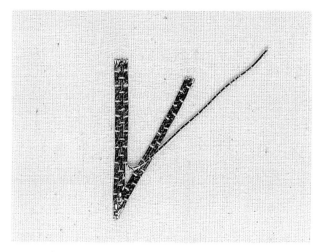

C *Couched gold threads with an acute corner.*

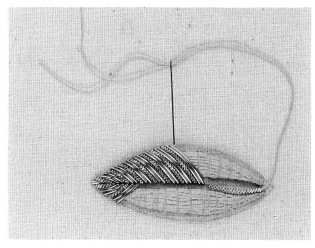

D *Purl gold threads sewn over padding as satin stitch (stage 1).*

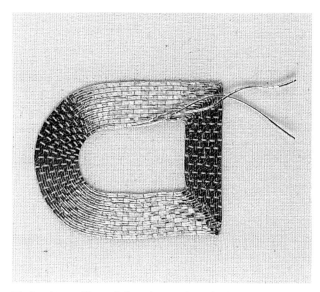

E *Couching gold. Stitch from the outside in, bricking the stitches.*

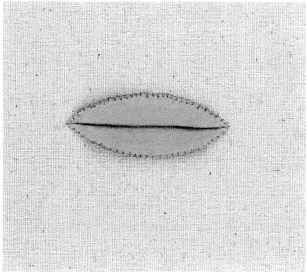

F *Purl gold threads sewn over padding as satin stitch (stage 2).*

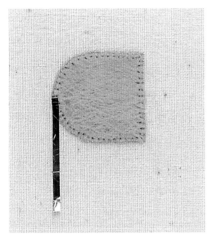

G *Plate application (stage 1).*

H *Plate application (stage 2).*

I *Plate application finished work.*

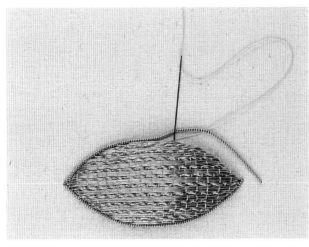

j *Couching Pearl Purl (stage 1).*

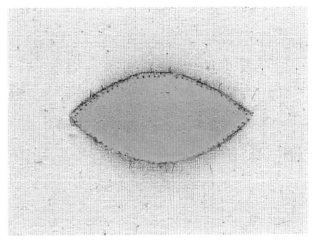

K *Couching Pearl Purl finished work.*

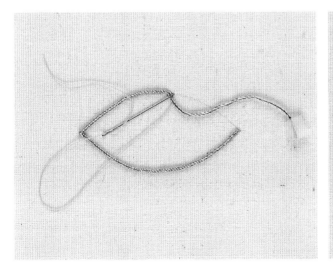

L *Sewing down Twist.*

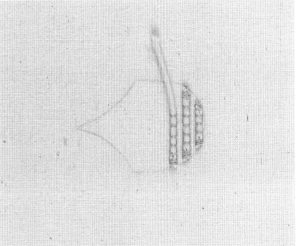

M *String padding.*

Padding techniques used for goldwork projects on pages 118–45.

(*Left row*) *Padding with felt using five layers, starting with the smallest one.*

(*Middle row*) *Padding with soft string, chamfering at the tip, covered with felt and stitched down the vein.*

(*Right row*) *Carpet felt for padding oversew down, finally covered with a layer of felt.*

LIST OF SUPPLIERS

Metallic threads and silk cottons and wools:

Royal School of Needlework
Apartment 12a
Hampton Court Palace
East Molesey
Surrey KT8 9AU

Mace & Nairn
89 Crane Street
Salisbury
Wiltshire SP1 2PY

Metal threads:

Janice Williams
Sheldon Cottage
Studio E
Epney
Saul
Gloucester GL2 7LN

Space dyed threads and fabric:

Steff Francis
Waverley
Higher Rocombe
Stoketeignhead
Newton Abbot
Devon
TQ12 4QL

Silks and fabric manipulation, metallic tissue:

Silk Route
32 Wolseley Road
Godalming
Surrey GU7 3EA

Interesting textured threads:

20th Century Yarns
73 The Thoroughfare
Woodbridge
Suffolk IP12 1AH
(mail order)

Manufacturers of gold thread:

Benton and Johnson
19-21 Great Queen Street
London WC2B 5BE

Embroidery threads:

Coats Crafts UK
PO Box 22
The Lingfield Estate
Mc Mullen Road
Darlington
Co. Durham DL1 1YQ

DMC Creative World plc
Pullman Road
Wigston
Leicester LE8 2DY

Dyes and paints:

Art Van Go
16 Hollybush Lane
Datchworth
Knebworth
Hertfordshire SG3 6RE

INDEX